DEAD ENDS

DEAD ENDS

B.C. Crime Stories

Paul Willcocks

University of Regina Press

Printed and bound in Canada at Friesens.
The text of this book is printed on 100% post-consumer recycled paper with earth-friendly vegetable based inks.

Cover and text design: Duncan Campbell, University of Regina Press.
Editor for the Press: David McLennan, University of Regina Press.
Copy editor: Anne James.
Cover photo: "portrait," © Grabi /iStockphoto.

LIBRARY AND ARCHIVES CANADA CATALOGUING IN PUBLICATION
Cataloguing in Publication (CIP) data available at the Library and Archives Canada web site: www.collectionscanada.gc.ca and at www.uofrpress.ca/publications/Dead-Ends

10   9   8   7   6   5   4   3   2   1

University of Regina Press, University of Regina
Regina, Saskatchewan, Canada, s4s 0A2
TEL: (306) 585-4758   FAX: (306) 585-4699
WEB: www.uofrpress.ca

The University of Regina Press acknowledges the support of the Creative Industry Growth and Sustainability program, made possible through funding provided to the Saskatchewan Arts Board by the Government of Saskatchewan through the Ministry of Parks, Culture, and Sport. We also acknowledge the financial support of the Government of Canada through the Canada Book Fund and the support of the Canada Council for the Arts for our publishing program.

CONTENTS

ACKNOWLEDGEMENTS

Researching this book provided a reminder of our shared debt to the people who gather our history while it happens, preserve the records through the years, and come up with new ways to make the information accessible.

Newspaper reporters and editors across British Columbia think of their jobs as providing information for readers of the next edition. But since 1858, they have been creating an invaluable historical record of events, and of society's attitudes.

Archivists, librarians, and historians have preserved and organized the original documents that make work like this possible—the court judgments, letters, wanted posters, scrawled notes, and photos.

We all owe them thanks.

Thanks also to Donna Grant and David McLennan and the University of Regina Press for the chance to work on this book.

And, most importantly, to Jody Paterson, for her encouragement, sharp editorial eye, and ability to make every day a new adventure.

INTRODUCTION

I was twenty-five when I spent six months as the police and court reporter for the *Red Deer Advocate*, and had a glimpse into another world. The stories were intense, tragic, funny, surprising—sometimes all at the same time. The characters, on both sides of the criminal divide, were compelling and complex, the best and worst of humanity on display every day.

And the crimes I covered sometimes turned out to reveal a great deal about the rest of us, and the society we live in.

The stories in this book span more than 150 years, from the high-profile and infamous to the almost forgotten. British Columbia has a rich tradition of outlaws, wrongdoing, and evil. The challenge was narrowing the list to forty crimes.

It was tempting to leave out people like Clifford Olson as too horrible or well-known. But it has been more than three decades since that summer of terror. We should not forget.

I looked for crimes that told us something about ourselves. Just as we should not forget Olson, we should not forget the entrenched racism that allowed a young man to be kidnapped by police agents because he was Chinese. Nor should we fail to recognize our shared role in denying the help that would have kept some of the people in the book from becoming victims, and others from becoming criminals.

And mostly I looked for crimes that were just darn good stories. That was the easy part. Bank robbers, con men, killers, and thieves lead fascinating, sometimes repellent, lives in a world most of us rarely get to see.

MILKSHAKE MURDERER

Rene Castellani stood above the city of Vancouver in the summer of 1965. Literally, as he waved to people on busy West Broadway from a car atop the twenty-nine-metre neon sign at BowMac Motors.

Within two years, he was sentenced to stand on a different kind of platform. A gallows.

Castellani was a star with CKNW. He was the Dizzy Dialer, king of prank calls and stunts, broadcasting live when the Beatles made their only Vancouver appearance in the summer of 1964. He fooled—and outraged—Vancouverites with another stunt, pretending to be an Indian maharajah who wanted to buy British Columbia, swathed in robes, surrounded by bodyguards and beautiful women.

In June 1965, he pledged to stay in a car atop BowMac's landmark neon sign until every vehicle on the lot sold. It took eight days. (The dealer's sales manager was a young go-getter named Jimmy Pattison, who went on to become a billionaire and one of British Columbia's most successful entrepreneurs.)

But while Castellani was waving to the crowds, his wife, Esther, was stricken in a hospital four blocks away, suffering from symptoms that baffled doctors.

By July 11, she was dead.

Who knows how Castellani, married almost nineteen years, got the idea. Maybe it was the times. The Beatles, Rolling Stones, The Who all released their first albums in 1964. Protests against the Vietnam War broke out. Ken Kesey and the Merry Pranksters set out in an old bus to bring LSD to America, and long-haired young people started arriving in San Francisco's Haight Ashbury. Castellani was forty, and no hippie. But maybe he decided the old rules didn't apply any more.

Or maybe it was just a more familiar story. A man wanted out of a marriage because he had met someone new, younger, prettier. And decided on a deadly solution.

And Rene almost got away with it.

It should have been a good time for the Castellani family.

Rene's career had finally taken off. Two years earlier, things had looked bleak. The family had to leave Campbell River, where Castellani was assistant manager of the Willows Hotel, when the historic building burned to the ground, killing four people. (Even then, Castellani was a promoter—when a resident reported seeing a "sea monster" off the city's waterfront, Castellani quickly offered a fifty-dollar reward for a photo, hoping to increase business at the hotel.)

In Vancouver, he found his niche. He was promotions manager at CKNW, the "Big Dog," as it billed itself, as well as an on-air personality. His wife, Esther, described as happy and upbeat by her manager, worked in a children's clothing store. With their twelve-year-old daughter, Jeannine, they lived in a tidy, one-storey duplex on a pleasant street in Kerrisdale, a pleasant neighbourhood then and now.

But behind the picture window that overlooked West 42nd Avenue, things were going terribly wrong.

Early in 1965, Esther received late-night anonymous calls from a woman who said her husband was "going around with someone else." He left early for work, but when she called, he wasn't there. And she found a love letter in his pocket from someone named Lolly.

Esther confronted Rene, who denied having an affair.

Soon after, Esther was struck by a mysterious illness. Stomach pains, then back pains and nausea and diarrhea. Her hands went numb, and she could scarcely lift a book or feed herself. She started to miss work, and made worried visits to doctors. Doctors ran through the usual suspects—gallbladder problems and other ailments were diagnosed, and ruled out.

And Esther became sicker, and sicker, with increasing visits to the hospital. Finally, early that summer, she was admitted for a long stay. Still, doctors were baffled.

Rene was the dutiful husband. He even brought Esther food he had prepared, at home and in the hospital, and her favourite White Spot vanilla milkshakes, one of the few things she could stomach as she got sicker and sicker.

But Rene Castellani, despite his denials, *was* having an affair. Lolly was the nickname of Adelaide Miller, a receptionist at CKNW. She was much younger than Rene and Esther, attractive and stylish, with upswept hair and artfully made-up eyes. And available—Lolly had been recently widowed when her husband drowned while they were boating.

Esther wasn't unattractive, with a friendly face and short, permed hair. But she was no Lolly.

The relationship began in the fall of 1964. Within months, the couple's lack of discretion was making waves at the station, and rumours spread quickly.

Lolly was fired in May because of the relationship; Rene was spared, supposedly because Esther was sick. (That Lolly, single mother of a six-year-old son, was not entitled to similar compassion says a lot about women's place in the workplace in 1964.)

Their recklessness would ultimately prove much more costly.

On July 11, 1965, five days before their wedding anniversary, Esther died. An autopsy at Vancouver General Hospital the next day found the cause was heart failure and an unknown viral infection. Her body was released, and buried two days later in Forest Lawn Memorial Park in Burnaby.

And Rene and Lolly might have lived happily ever after.

Except the case nagged at Dr. Bernard Moscovich, the internist who had cared for Esther. He wanted—needed—to know why she had died. And after poring over the charts and evidence, he concluded something toxic had killed her, perhaps arsenic. He ordered tests on tissue samples—and the results found lethal quantities of arsenic, hundreds of times the normal levels.

Moscovich reported the findings to police, and they searched the Castellani home and found a box of Triox weed killer under the kitchen sink. The main ingredient—arsenic.

On August 3, Esther's body was exhumed from its concrete vault, and an examination confirmed poisoning by arsenic, administered over a period of months.

There was still no direct link to Rene. But police suspicions were certainly heightened when they found Rene had left on a Disneyland holiday with Lolly, her son, and his daughter five days after his wife's death. And that the couple had already applied for a loan to buy a house together.

Police began building a case. They learned of the affair, the long, lingering illness, the arsenic poisoning, and the unseemly activities of Lolly and Rene after Esther's death. (By September, they were living together.)

And witnesses began recalling those milkshakes Rene had encouraged Esther to drink every day, the meals he sometimes brought to the hospital—and the way the milkshake containers and any leftovers always seemed to disappear when he left.

The noose was tightening. CKNW fired Castellani in October. In December, a three-day inquest heard about the affair, the arsenic poisoning, and the partially emptied box of weed killer under the sink. And the inquest jurors heard about the milkshakes, and the way the containers always disappeared from the hospital room.

Coroners' juries can't assign guilt. But someone killed Esther, they concluded.

It was just a matter of time after that. Rene was charged with murdering Esther on April 7, 1966, just days after he and Lolly had applied for a marriage licence. He couldn't make the $15,000 bail.

The trial began on October 31, 1966—Halloween. He pleaded not guilty. But over nine days, and with more than forty prosecution witnesses, the case was built against Castellani. Witnesses described the suspicious milkshakes, and a nurse testified that Rene had given her a ride home and casually asked when she thought Esther would die—a question she found chilling from a supposedly concerned husband.

Other witnesses testified about the affair, and that Rene and Lolly had told them about their marriage plans even before Esther was dead.

That, the prosecutor said, explained the motive. In 1965, divorce in British Columbia was still covered by the terms of the British Matrimonial Causes Act of 1857. Unless Esther was cheating, or guilty of cruelty to Rene, he couldn't divorce her. She wasn't. The marriage plans meant Rene knew he was going to kill his wife, they argued.

Doctors and experts testified the arsenic was administered over at least five months, ruling out some one-time mishap. The poisoning was consistent with Triox, the weed killer found under the kitchen sink. (Its presence was never explained; Triox killed everything, including lawns. It was for clearing brush, not tidying a home garden.)

And analyst Eldon Rideout testified that Esther's hair samples showed a significant drop in the amount of poison she was consuming during the eight days Castellani was atop the auto dealer's sign.

That could have been good news for defence lawyer Al Mackoff. If Esther had been given arsenic while Rene was on top of a giant sign for a week, he couldn't have been the killer.

But prosecutor P. G. Bowen-Colthurst quickly produced witnesses to confirm that Rene hadn't really remained on top of the sign, slipping down regularly and even visiting Esther in hospital. Even the landmark publicity stunt was a hoax.

Rene didn't testify. The defence called no witnesses. It took the jury, twelve men in suits, four hours to find him guilty, and only ten minutes to decide against leniency—meaning Castellani should hang for the crime.

It wasn't over. He appealed, saying the judge had made errors in instructing the jury. The British Columbia Court of Appeal agreed, and ordered a new trial.

When it began, on September 25, 1967, new defence lawyer Charles Maclean tried a different approach. Castellani took the stand and denied killing Esther, pleading his complete innocence. His daughter, also a defence witness, testified that an aunt had threatened to kill her mother.

But the doctors and the analysts and the nurses and the friends told the story.

It took the jury a bit longer—six hours of deliberation. But Rene was again found guilty, and again sentenced to death.

Castellani appealed to the British Columbia Court of Appeal and the Supreme Court of Canada to overturn the verdict. Both turned him down.

But Rene was spared the noose. In 1967, under then prime minister Lester Pearson, the government introduced legislation providing for a five-year moratorium on capital punishment. (The death penalty was abolished in 1976.)

Instead, Rene Castellani went to prison, and stayed there until 1979.

He always maintained his innocence. And he remained convincing. After being released from jail, he went back into the radio business, first in Abbotsford and then as promotions manager at Nanaimo's CKEG, a new country radio station trying to break into the market. He was even married again—though not to Lolly.

But freedom was short-lived. Castellani died of cancer on January 4, 1982, in Nanaimo.

It had been a long, hard fall from his perch on the top of the BowMac sign.

CRAZY EDDIE

They called him Crazy Eddie in the Okanagan Valley.

Eddie Haymour complained constantly that powerful forces were conspiring against him, plotting to steal his land and his dreams, ruining his life.

The provincial government, police, and bureaucrats were part of the conspiracy, he'd tell anyone who would listen.

By 1972, most people dismissed the former barber as paranoid, a nut.

But Haymour was right. Powerful politicians and bureaucrats *were* conspiring against him, using and abusing the courts and coercion to kill his dream and force him to sell his beloved Lake Okanagan island to the government at a desperately cheap price.

What nobody realized was how far Eddie would go to get justice.

Haymour was an outsider in the small Okanagan community of Peachland, about thirty minutes south of Kelowna, when he came to pursue his vision of the Canadian dream in 1970.

He was born forty years earlier in the Beqaa Valley of Lebanon, an area of rich farmlands, hills and lakes, and spectacular Roman ruins. His family—his Muslim father and Christian mother—decided to move to Beirut when he was a young man, and Haymour became a barber.

But he wanted more. And in 1955, he emigrated to Canada, where his sister was already living. Haymour didn't speak English, and arrived with seventeen dollars in his pocket. He got a sign that said "Me Barber," learned to pronounce the two words, and walked around Edmonton until he got work.

Haymour worked hard, with tremendous energy. He started his own barbershop, bought a home, and opened hair salons and stylist schools in Calgary and Edmonton. It was the Canadian dream.

He was charming, handsome, captured in a photo in white tux and black bow tie, a cigarette in one hand, black hair shiny and swept back, a strong cleft chin.

In 1960, when he became a Canadian citizen, Haymour was so proud that he threw a lavish Mideast-themed celebration for 250 people, complete with belly dancers. Edmonton mayor Elmer Roper and the lieutenant governor were on the guest list. "The best day of my life," he recalled later.

But as he neared his forties, Haymour started to reflect on his life. He had married a Canadian, Loreen, and they had four children. But Haymour worked constantly and the marriage was increasingly strained.

It was time for a change.

In 1970, Haymour decided the Okanagan Valley offered a new start. With the fruit trees and gentle hills surrounding the large lake, it reminded him of the Beqaa Valley.

The Okanagan was a conservative place in 1970. Kelowna had 19,000 residents, less than one-sixth today's population.

Haymour—with his Lebanese background, self-made wealth, and a big personality—stood out. Especially when he built his dream house on a rocky ridge overlooking the lake. It was enormous, and defied architectural labels, part Moorish castle and part German chateau.

The site offered spectacular views across the valley. Which meant the towering house, with seven bedrooms, three living rooms, and two elevators, was visible for miles. People called it an eyesore, sniffed at the ostentation.

Haymour had more plans. He dreamed of a Mideast-themed amusement park to bring people to the Okanagan. On a Sunday afternoon drive, he spotted Rattlesnake Island, in front of Peachland. It was empty, just rock and scrub and grass, and, at 1.8 hectares, a perfect place to build his dream.

Haymour was a doer. He found out the unzoned property could be developed any way he wanted. He presented his ideas to Peachland council, which agreed to help with an onshore dock for the water taxis that would ferry visitors to his attraction.

And he bought the island, drafted his plans, and started building. Haymour didn't hire architects; he walked the island and started sketching—a dock to welcome visitors here, an eighteen-hole miniature golf course, each hole celebrating a different aspect of Mideastern culture, here, two pyramids, a swimming pool, restaurants serving delicacies from his home-land, a twelve-metre-tall concrete camel children could play inside, a cave, and a pretend submarine.

But some well-connected locals weren't happy—including W. A. C. Bennett, the legendary Social Credit premier who represented the riding.

Suddenly, Haymour started having problems. Approvals he needed for things like a sewage system were stalled in the bureaucracy. The Highways Ministry blocked access to the ferry dock. The provincial government retroactively zoned the island as "'a forest and grazing reserve," even though it only had one tree.

When he tried to welcome several hundred guests to a pre-view in June 1972, RCMP officers spent the day at the water taxi dock discouraging people from attending.

Haymour pressed on, despite the enormous challenges and mounting costs. He became increasingly convinced he was the victim of a conspiracy.

But the Royal Bank heard about the problems and delays and pulled his loans.

The project was dead, and the $170,000 he had spent on it was lost. Haymour couldn't pay his bills. His marriage, not surprisingly, began to fall apart, and in July 1973 Loreen and the children moved back to Alberta. The government made a lowball offer of $40,000 for the island.

But Haymour wouldn't sell. He complained of the con-spiracy, pleaded for help from anyone he could reach, even fly-ing back to ask the Lebanese government to intervene. No one believed him. In fact, people thought he was nuts.

But Haymour was right. Behind the scenes, Bennett, provincial cabinet ministers, local officials, and at least six government departments had been secretly conspiring to make sure the project would never be built.

Then Haymour went too far. He started to talk about using violence to force the government to address his case. The RCMP put him under surveillance, and an undercover officer befriended him and listened to his angry rants.

On December 19, 1973, police arrested Haymour and Crown prosecutors laid thirty-seven criminal charges, including manufacturing letter bombs, plotting to blow up a bridge, and conspiring to hijack an airplane. He spent six months in jail awaiting his day in court, passing some of the time by trimming other inmates' hair.

Prison was a nightmare. He learned Loreen was filing for divorce and the bank was foreclosing on the island. His dream home was destroyed in a suspicious fire. The insurance renewal form hadn't reached him in jail, so he had no coverage.

When he finally appeared for trial, thirty-six of the charges were dropped. All that remained was a charge for possession of lightweight brass knuckles, something that never would have resulted in his detention before trial.

Haymour wanted to plead guilty, which would have allowed him to walk out of court a free man.

But the Crown pressed for a verdict of not guilty by reason of insanity. Court-ordered psychiatrists testified Haymour was delusional, believing "there was a conspiracy on behalf of certain people in the government to thwart his business attempts."

The fact that his beliefs might be true apparently never crossed anyone's mind. The judge found Haymour insane and ordered him committed.

During a recess in the hearing, government representatives pressed him again—sign over the property for $40,000. Desperate to end the process and hoping the government would then leave him alone, he agreed.

"They adjourned it for 15 minutes and they brought me the paper and asked me to sign," Haymour said later. "I would have sold it back for a dollar, anything to get the hell out of there."

The transaction was illegal and unconscionable, a British Columbia Supreme Court justice would later rule. How could government officials argue Haymour was insane and press him to sell his property to them at the same time?

Haymour spent eleven months in Riverview mental institution before being released in 1975, planning to return to Lebanon. (He believed leaving Canada was a condition of his release.)

After four years of struggle, most people would have given up.

But Haymour raised the stakes. He enlisted some cousins in Beirut, got his hands on machine guns and, on February 26, 1976, stormed into the Canadian Embassy and took about two dozen hostages. After a nine-hour standoff, his key demands were granted—amnesty for the hostage-taking, and a return to Canada so he could press his case for compensation.

Haymour settled down. But he didn't give up. He built a small house, borrowed money from a few friends, and tried to interest a lawyer in his case. He finally found a dedicated champion in lawyer Jack Cram, a skillful advocate for the underdog and eccentric, always willing to take on the establishment.

It took ten years, but on August 7, 1986, Haymour walked into the British Columbia Supreme Court in Vancouver and waited nervously for the verdict in his lawsuit against the government, after a trial that had stretched over eight months.

Justice Gordon MacKinnon delivered a devastating judgment, concluding the government had conspired against Haymour and harassed him into poverty and a mental institution.

"I am satisfied senior officials of government, including ministers of the Crown and with the knowledge of the premier (W. A. C. Bennett) contrived to improperly curb Haymour's development," MacKinnon wrote in a seventy-five-page judgment. Pressing him to sell the property at a low price during his criminal proceedings was unconscionable.

At least six government departments were part of the conspiracy, MacKinnon found. The actions had been "highly improper, illegal and even cruel."

And the government was not content with shutting down the project, the judgment noted, but conspired to drive "the price of the property down through the use of regulation, and effectively drove the plaintiff to the brink of financial disaster."

The government could have expropriated the island at any time, he added.

Haymour was awarded the difference between the price the government paid and the property's real value, plus interest—about $155,000. The scandal led to an investigation by the provincial ombudsman, and his report brought another $140,000 and a public apology from the government.

Haymour was fifty-six. His second marriage had collapsed and he had been through hell, but he still had his dreams.

With the settlement, he built Casa Haymour, a bed and breakfast and restaurant that was a mini-version of his planned theme park. He sometimes greeted guests in flowing Arab-style robes.

His view included Rattlesnake Island, by then part of a provincial park. Haymour, with a sweeping moustache and thick glasses, could look out at the island and think about what might have been.

THE INDIAN PROBLEM

The invitations went out quietly, secretly, in the fall of 1921. Words were whispered in the longhouses and Native communities on British Columbia's central coast, as the forests shone in the rain.

'Namgis Chief Dan Cranmer was preparing to host a potlatch on Village Island. A time to gather, to bring out sacred masks and robes and share the foods and gifts he would provide.

A time to sing and dance the old stories.

But it had to be secret. The Canadian government had made potlatches illegal, and police were waiting to pounce.

Cranmer had a wedding to celebrate. More than that, there was a culture to keep alive. The Kwakwaka'wakw people had no written language. They shared their history, their beliefs, through stories and songs at gatherings like potlatches.

Winter was a traditional time for potlatches. The salmon and herring and oolichan would not be in the rivers for months. People had time and could gather for celebrations.

Or once they could. They could share the old stories, and pass them on to their children. They could outdo each other with gifts and feasts.

But in 1884, the Canadian Parliament had passed a law to make potlatches illegal. The Indian agents and missionaries complained potlatches were wasteful. The government believed potlatches helped keep alive a culture that needed to be eradicated if Indians were to give up their past and become English-speaking, Christian subjects of the British Crown.

Since potlatches were banned, Cranmer would risk prison for giving gifts to guests. Participating in dancing and singing or sharing the stories was a crime, punishable by at least two months, and up to six years, in prison.

At first, the laws were much ignored, with judges reluctant to impose penalties when charges were filed.

But in 1913, fifty nine-year-old Duncan Campbell Scott became superintendent general of the Department of Indian Affairs.

Scott, a career Indian Affairs bureaucrat, was a fervent advocate of forced assimilation. "I want to get rid of the Indian problem," he wrote. "Our objective is to continue until there is not a single Indian in Canada that has not been absorbed into the body politic and there is no Indian question, and no Indian Department." (Scott was also a poet and writer; his literary reputation has been overshadowed by his role in implementing Indian residential schools.)

Potlatches kept the culture alive. Scott wanted them stopped.

And if the courts wouldn't do it, he had another plan. Scott persuaded the government to make the crimes summary offences. That meant judges no longer heard the cases. Indian agents could hear the evidence as justices of the peace and render verdicts. They worked for Scott. They knew what their masters wanted.

Cranmer's local adversary was William Halliday, the newly appointed Indian agent for Alert Bay, who shared Scott's zeal for ending the potlatch culture.

Cranmer was thirty-three, a handsome and respected leader. He knew the risks and made plans to avoid Halliday and the police. His people had been induced to move from their traditional village on the Nimpkish River to Alert Bay, then a growing town on northern Vancouver Island.

It wasn't safe to hold a potlatch there, with so many watch-white eyes. Cranmer planned to hold the ceremony on Vil-Island, near Knight Inlet, far from the church and the ment agents and the police.

potlatch was a great success. Representatives from ve bands made their way to Village Island, carrying their potlatch regalia and sacred items. The gifts were lavish, part of a tradition of competitive sharing that saw each host and clan strive to outdo the next. Guests received gas-powered boats, pool tables, sewing machines, gramophones, cash, and blankets.

"The potlatch went on for five or six days," Dan Cranmer's son Bill told the Victoria *Times Colonist* in 2005. "It was apparently one of the biggest potlatches ever held in our area."

Too big, perhaps. Word had reached the authorities.

Halliday and Sgt. Donald Angerman of the British Columbia Police travelled across the water to Village Island and found the potlatch in full swing. They immediately started arresting participants.

Forty-five people were charged and brought before Halliday as justice of the peace. Angerman was the prosecutor.

There they were offered a choice. Be sent to Oakalla Prison for two to four months.

Or give up the masks and robes and whistles and art that were part of their culture and essential to celebrating the potlatch. Not just their own items. To avoid jail for their members, the bands would have to surrender all those things that linked the people to their past, and let them share their history.

Twenty-two people said yes. Oakalla was a fearsome place for Natives who had never left the coast. The struggle to keep the old ways alive had become, for many, just too hard.

The rest—men and women—were led away in front of crying relatives to be locked up in the jail outside Vancouver, clearing trees, working the prison farm, sleeping on straw mattresses in crowded cells.

"Great Potlatch May Be Last Of Its Kind," said the headline in the *British Colonist*, a Victoria newspaper: "Chief Dan Cranmer's Festival Somewhat Marred By Interference Of Authorities."

Soon Natives began arriving in Alert Bay, handing over masks and robes and copper engravings and rattles, the potlatch art and regalia handed down within the tribe.

They gave up hundreds of pieces of art and craft, the links to their past and their culture. The carved masks and robes worn by dancers were spectacular, eagles and thunderbirds and spirits. They were beautiful, and valuable.

Halliday displayed all the seized goods on benches in the Alert Bay Anglican Parish Hall and charged admission for people who wanted to see them. A keen amateur photographer, he and others set out to record the masks and robes and regalia.

The public exhibit was another cruel blow to the First Nations, who believed the artifacts were sacred and kept them stored out of sight in cedar boxes when they were not being used.

Halliday struck a deal to sell thirty-three items to George Heye, a New York collector. The pieces, with the rest of Heye's collection, were displayed in his newly opened Museum of the American Indian in New York City, made a part of the Smithsonian Institution in 1990.

Most of the carvings and art were crated up and shipped east. About half went to the Victoria Memorial Museum in Ottawa, a predecessor of today's Canadian Museum of History, and half to the Royal Ontario Museum in Toronto.

And some were just taken. Scott picked some pieces for his personal collection. So did Angerman, the arresting officer and prosecutor when the natives were pressured to give up their cultural treasures.

But on Vancouver Island, the pieces were never forgotten. And in 1951, when the potlatch laws were removed from the Indian Act, efforts began to recover the items seized three decades earlier.

It took time, and tremendous persistence from the Kwakwaka'wakw. Museums are sensitive about how their collections have been acquired, fearing a long list of repatriation requests.

The National Museum of Man—the 1970s incarnation of today's Canadian Museum of History—was first to agree that the Kwakwaka'wakw had been wrongly forced to give up their ceremonial masks and robes and art. But it insisted that a proper museum to house the collection be built on their territory before returning the collection.

The bulk of the collection was from the 'Namgis Band and the Cape Mudge Band. Each wanted the items in its own community. By 1974, they agreed to build two museums and allow descendants of the original owners to decide where their artifacts should reside. Funding from national museum programs supported the two projects.

The Royal Ontario Museum returned its items in 1988, and the Smithsonian in 1994. A woman from France personally delivered a headdress that had been in her father's office for decades.

That left one holdout—the British Museum, which steadfastly refused to give up its transformation mask, a carving of a crest that opened to reveal a face. British law makes it illegal for the British Museum to return items.

But U'mista Cultural Centre executive director Andrea Sanborn was not deterred. She showed up at one meeting at the British Museum with an empty Adidas bag. It's to bring the mask home in, she told the puzzled directors. By 2005, she had negotiated a solution. The British Museum would retain ownership, but loan the mask to its original owners.

For the Kwakwaka'wakw, a part of their culture was restored.

They celebrated with a potlatch.

THE BIG CON

Everything about Ian Thow was big.

The investment adviser's house was a $5.5-million waterfront mansion outside Victoria, with four bedrooms and seven bathrooms. There was a dock on the Saanich Inlet for his yacht, a seventeen-metre Sea Ray that would sleep six, and two smaller boats.

The seven-acre property had a pad for Thow's Jet Ranger helicopter. There was a shiny collection of cars—four Mercedes, two Escalades, a Porsche, a Corvette, and more.

And Thow had a fleet of three airplanes, including a $12-million Citation X that could carry nine and was the fastest non-military aircraft in the world. He used it to ferry investment clients to lavish weekend getaways.

Ian Thow was big—six foot three and over 200 pounds—with a big head, ruddy face, and hair cropped close at the sides. He seemed to be everywhere in Victoria, raising money for charities, pledging big chunks of his own cash for causes, front and centre at every gala, bidding enthusiastically at the charity auctions that were part of the social scene for the people with money.

But biggest of all, it turned out, were Thow's lies.

Ian Thow had a flair for self-publicity, and a confidence and boldness rare in quiet Victoria.

Thow started getting noticed in 1993, when he was promoted to manager of the local Investors Group office at thirty-three, a coup for a young salesman.

He started to indulge a penchant for living large—building a profile, going to the right events, attracting media attention. He pledged money to charitable causes, organized dinners for the homeless, hung out with police, and led the Crime Stoppers program.

But Thow was still just a mutual fund salesman, one whose last business effort, a travel agency, had ended in bankruptcy. A good salesman—and Thow was a great salesman—could earn an excellent living selling investments to people looking for a comfortable retirement.

But not enough money to pay for yachts and flashy charitable donations and a seat at the social-circuit table with Victoria's old money.

Don Jenson, Thow's former supervisor at Investors, had recommended the promotion to branch manager. But Thow's spending surprised him. "I could see his lifestyle changing. He was driving bigger cars and he bought a yacht, which I couldn't afford as a regional manager. People began asking questions."

When Thow suddenly resigned from Investors in 1998, it made the local business pages, along with questions about his next move.

A month later, Thow announced he would be heading British Columbia operations for Toronto-based Berkshire Investment Group. Founder Michael Lee-Chin, starting with $400, had used the investment company to become a billionaire.

Thow expanded the Berkshire office, and kept up his literally high-flying lifestyle, while building a media profile as a businessman and philanthropist.

All that charitable work kept him in the news. And built trust.

He was always there, ready to shave his head for Cops for Cancer if business friends would donate $20,000, or race shopping carts to raise money for a food bank.

And he was a big friend of the police. After one of Thow's "ride-alongs" with officers, he decided to raise $100,000 to buy the Victoria Police Department a boat for marine operations. "It actually took me about two hours to raise the money,'" he boasted.

The charitable operations kept getting bigger. Thow said he raised $1.1 million for a special fund at the Royal Roads University Foundation to honour Alex Campbell, the founder of Thrifty Foods grocery chain, and a highly respected business leader on Vancouver Island. He created the Greater Victoria Police Foundation and announced $2 million in donations to provide better equipment for officers.

When former NHL players Russ and Geoff Courtnall launched a campaign to raise money for mental health services—their father had committed suicide—Thow jumped in. He pledged $100,000, donated the use of his yacht, and stood up at a gala dinner to announce that he would offer an auction item—a trip to Maui on his private jet and a stay in a luxury hotel. But only if one of the celebrities at the dinner agreed to go with the high bidder. Nickelback's Chad Kroeger and Keifer Sutherland both stepped up, and the package went for $35,000.

"We thought he was a paragon of virtue," a client said later. "He was running Crime Stoppers and he was always donating to these various charities, and he just seemed, like, you know, the man of the hour."

Thow flaunted his success and wealth. He flew clients and prospects off to the $1,100-a-day West Coast Fishing Club, or on wildly lavish weekends in Las Vegas, where he bought the most expensive wines, even a $10,000 bottle of Scotch.

And he made much of his friendship with billionaire Lee-Chin, and his title of senior vice-president and member of the Berkshire advisory board.

No one looked too hard at how Thow—still really a mutual fund salesman—was finding all this money.

Even when Thow started offering some clients, including ones dissatisfied with the performance of the funds he had sold them, a chance to make huge returns with "special investments."

Some were offered a chance to make short-term loans to Vancouver developers. Safe, secure, and a ten-percent return in just three months, Thow promised.

Thow told others of a hot opportunity. He could help them buy shares in the National Commercial Bank of Jamaica. Lee-

Chin had bought majority control in 2002; big things were about to happen.

There were other stories, other offers, all alluring.

All the deals had two things in common. The cheques were to be made out to Thow, or his personal company, not Berkshire.

And the investments didn't exist.

Thow used charm and persuasion—and the trust created by his public persona—to gut his victims, getting every dollar possible.

Shirley Garwood and Helena Kells were typical. Thow had managed their money for years, and they had followed him from the Investors Group to Berkshire. He visited them at home, called them his "favourite ladies," and told them he would always look out for them.

In 2004, Garwood was sixty-five and Kells was seventy-seven. They were worried about the poor performance of the mutual funds Thow had sold them.

And he offered a solution—short-term loans to developers, safe and lucrative.

They had no money. But Thow said they could sell their Berkshire investments, cash in their RRSPs, and mortgage the house they shared.

And the sisters, living on fixed incomes, did, handing $465,000 to Thow after he repeatedly visited their home and pressed his case.

Investor after investor later told of accepting Thow's advice to remortgage their homes or open giant lines of credit. He had an in at Scotiabank and could get loans even for people with little income and no prospects for repayment. One client got $50,000 to give to Thow, when other banks wouldn't even approve his credit card applications.

It wasn't just the easily conned. Alex Campbell—the business leader Thow supposedly honoured by raising $1.1 million for a university endowment—ultimately trusted Thow with $12 million. Tom Harris, who owned five car dealerships and a chain of cellphone stores across British Columbia and Alberta, invested hundreds of thousands of dollars.

Thow had crafted a stellar reputation, and had an uncanny gift for judging what would work with each mark—a Vegas weekend, an apparent interest in helping with personal troubles, flattery.

When people got nervous or asked questions, Thow put them off, or told them he had reinvested the money so they would make even more. Pressed hard enough, he would come up with some of the money or fly them to Jamaica to see the bank meeting with Lee-Chin.

But it couldn't last. In September 2004, a lawyer who had done work for Berkshire heard a disturbing tale on the golf course.

Lou Vavaroutsos, owner of successful car dealerships around Toronto, said Thow had invited him and other dealers to go salmon fishing. They had been talked into putting in at least $2 million for shares in the National Bank of Jamaica. Now they couldn't get Thow to deliver the shares or their money.

The lawyer called a former Berkshire senior manager. He called company executives, including Lee-Chin, to alert them. And he called Thow.

Thow was a fixer. You can have your money back, he told Vavaroutsos. But only if you tell Berkshire the golf course complaint was a misunderstanding. Berkshire's internal investigation was anemic.

That bought time. Time that Thow used to steal money from more people.

Seven months later, though, there was another, similar, complaint. Thow tried to stall and negotiated a deal to repay the money in return for silence. But he knew more disgruntled "investors" would soon be coming forward.

Summoned to a meeting with Berkshire brass in Toronto, Thow refused to answer most questions and resigned. The company agreed to postpone the official date of his resignation for a month and conducted no further investigations. (Although in later public statements Berkshire claimed it was investigating.)

The floodgates opened. People who had given money to Thow started suing. By Canada Day in 2005, four groups had filed suits claiming they had lost $2.9 million.

It was the tip of the iceberg. By the end of the month, that had climbed to $42 million.

And those big charitable donations turned out to be hot air. More than two years after Thow was feted for raising $1.1 million to honour Campbell, the Royal Roads University Foundation admitted it had received only $77,000. Media reports that Thow had raised $2 million for the police foundation were false. Even a $500,000 pledge to a hospital foundation that Thow had said was in memory of his mother went unpaid.

A blizzard of lawsuits was filed as Thow and creditors fought in court. The RCMP and the British Columbia Securities Commission launched investigations.

And then Thow vanished. On September 8, four days before he was supposed to present a bankruptcy plan, Thow loaded two trucks with TVs and other possessions and crossed the U.S. border at Blaine, Washington, after midnight. The RCMP had asked to be alerted if he tried to leave the country. But by the time an officer made the forty-five-minute drive from Vancouver, Thow was gone.

It was another blow for Thow's victims. Their lives had been shattered and savings built over decades stolen. There were divorces, depression, lost homes, lost trust, lost confidence.

And Thow was living in luxury condos, first in downtown Seattle, then in Portland's trendy Pearl District. He was driving new SUVs, flying to Las Vegas and Jamaica. The investors couldn't get at any money, but Thow could.

Incredibly, he even found work as a mortgage broker in Seattle—a job that gave him access to the financial information of a new set of prospective victims.

Less incredibly, Thow continued to spin a web of lies. He told a neighbour in Portland that he was a retired Microsoft executive, pals with Bill Gates, and had a twenty-one-metre yacht and homes in Seattle, Aspen, Mexico, and the Caribbean.

Back in Canada, his victims waited. And waited. The British Columbia Securities Exchange hearing on the fraud didn't happen until more than two years after Thow fled the country. Berkshire was eventually fined $500,000 for failing to investigate when first warned of problems. The company's neglect allowed Thow to steal another $6.3 million. Thow was fined $6 million, reduced to $250,000 on his appeal. It didn't matter; he would never pay.

The RCMP and prosecutors were even slower. It was not until June 26, 2008, three years after Thow had been exposed, that he was charged with twenty-five counts of fraud over $5,000. It took another eight months before United States marshals arrested Thow as he prepared to set out on a morning jog.

And it wasn't until March 1, 2010, almost five years after Thow fled the country, that he finally pleaded guilty and was sentenced to nine years in jail.

But white-collar criminals—even ones who show no remorse—don't stay in jail long. Thow got double credit for time served in custody before his plea, and was released on full parole less than three years after he was sent to jail.

For his victims, the damage will last a lifetime.

WOMEN WE KILLED

The pictures of Marnie Frey should break your heart. The grinning kid with the auburn hair and faded white shirt, about eight, posing beside her pet rabbit in its hay-filled cardboard box.

Or the girl a few years older, long legs sticking out of blue shorts, growing into a teen, smiling for the camera as her dad stands beside her with a forty-pound salmon from the waters around Campbell River.

Or the school photo of fourteen-year-old Marnie in 1987, big hair, dyed much lighter, and a bigger smile, despite a mouthful of braces.

You can see the carefree girl who loved animals, went shopping with her grandmother, laughed with her classmates at the Campbell River Christian School.

The girl who, ten years later, addicted and on the streets of the Downtown Eastside, would die at the hands of Robert "Willie" Pickton, the nightmarish Coquitlam pig farmer who killed some forty-nine women.

The girl who died because police, government, and most of us had decided she didn't count. Like all the others.

* * *

Campbell River, on Vancouver Island, was a fine place to live when Marnie was born on August 30, 1973.

The setting was stunning—pine forests and snow-capped mountains to the west, and the Strait of Georgia, Desolation Sound, and the Coast Range to the east. The forest industry, mills and mines, and the rich fishery provided high-paying jobs.

Marnie's dad, Rick Frey, was a commercial fisherman. Rick split with her mother, an Aboriginal woman, when Marnie was young. He raised her, taking her fishing, hunting, and camping, buying the pets she loved.

Her stepmom, Lynn, remembers a happy, active Marnie. "She was energetic, full of life, loved people, loved animals. She was nothing different than any other 14-year-old. She loved animals, she loved chickens, she loved birds. Her favourite bird was the eagle. She thought they were a free spirit as she was. She liked arts and crafts; she climbed trees. She did everything a child would do."

Marnie was generous—if a classmate needed new clothes, she would hand over her own.

But by 1987, resource towns like Campbell River had discovered drugs. At fourteen, Marnie was using hash and pot and, before long, cocaine. She left school in grade eleven, had a baby at nineteen. She named her Brittney; she loved that little girl.

Marnie managed to look after her daughter for a couple of years—a "damn good mum," Rick recalls. But she decided it would be best for Brittney to be raised by Rick and Lynn. They agreed to adopt. Brittney grew up thinking Marnie was her older sister.

The drugs though, they had a strong pull. Marnie kept using and got into debt with some Campbell River dealers when Brittney was three. She fled to Vancouver.

And things got rougher. Marnie was living in the Balmoral Hotel, once respectable, now a drug-infested dive in the heart-breaking Downtown Eastside, spending a friend's inheritance. She discovered heroin.

When Lynn asked Marnie where she got the money for drugs, she told the truth.

"I'm selling myself—it's really scary."

Marnie tried rehab several times, but couldn't face her fears of detox pains.

Through it all, she stayed in touch with Lynn and Rick and Brittney. She called home almost every day, often more than once, asking how her little girl was doing.

That ended after August 30, 1997, Marnie's twenty-fourth birthday. Lynn talked to Marnie for what turned out to be the last time, wished her a happy birthday. She had sent a birthday package—new clothes, homemade bread, and fifty dollars— and expected a call in the next few days from Marnie.

It never came. Lynn and Rick knew something was wrong. They tried to report their daughter missing, but the RCMP sent them away. It took five months to convince police to list Marnie as a missing person.

People like her, like all the women Pickton preyed on, went missing all the time, police said. Marnie would turn up.

That's one reason Pickton could kill again and again and again—forty-nine times—without getting caught. No one was even looking for the women he murdered.

If Marnie had been a university student and disappeared without a trace, police would have been searching for her.

But she was a sex worker and an addict. "They didn't give a damn," said Lynn Frey.

So Lynn started searching. It's almost five hours, by road and ferry, to Vancouver from Campbell River, but Lynn repeated the journey a couple of times a month, walking the streets of the Downtown Eastside, showing Marnie's picture and asking for information.

"I looked in Dumpsters, terrible places. I called morgues and hospitals. The police were not looking for her so I had to."

Vancouver's Downtown Eastside had become home to the desperate and damaged—addicts and the mentally ill and the lost. Its sidewalks showcased every kind of suffering, every day.

Lynn started to hear whispers about a man named "Willie," hunting women from the streets, killing them one by one.

A year after Marnie vanished, Lynn learned more. A sex worker said Marnie was dead. Murdered, and her body had been put through a wood chipper on a muddy farm about forty-five minutes from the Eastside.

Just weeks later, Lynn met a Downtown Eastside community worker who had taped a conversation with another sex worker. She said "Willie" had taken women to his pig farm and the chipper, and they would never be found again. Everyone on the street knew a serial killer was hunting women.

Lynn shared the story with a relative from Port Coquitlam, a Vancouver suburb. She knew about a pig farmer named "Willie," with a chipper on his muddy, messy property, and a shed called the Piggy Palace, the scene of wild, drunken parties.

They drove to the farm late one night and tried to scale the fence, but were scared away by Pickton's dogs. "That night when I went there, when I was backing out of the driveway, I had a very weird feeling…. She was there."

So Lynn went to the police and told them what she had learned.

And they did nothing. Lynn went back to the farm at least a dozen more times. That was all she could do for Marnie.

Pickton, he went on killing. It would be more than three years—and a dozen more murders—before police raided the farm on a firearms warrant and arrested him.

It was another two years, after a multi-million-dollar forensic search, until police called Rick Frey and said they had found part of Marnie's jawbone and four of her teeth on the farm.

In 2002, Robert "Willie" Pickton was charged with twenty-six counts of murder. He told an undercover police officer posing as a fellow inmate that he had killed forty-nine women.

In December 2007, he was convicted of six murder charges—including killing Marnie Frey—and sentenced to life in prison. The investigation and trial cost $115 million.

An inquiry into the missing women cost another $10 million.

It found police didn't act on clear evidence that a serial killer was preying on Vancouver women. The victims didn't matter. They were disposable.

Police, government, society didn't really care if they were killed. Pickton could have been stopped years earlier.

The pictures of Marnie Frey should break your heart.

OFFICERS DOWN

George Booth was odd.

But no one expected that in less than an hour he would turn a hot, dry coulee in Kamloops into a killing field. And that three young Mounties would be killed on a June morning in 1962.

Booth was thirty-one. He lived in a two-room shack in Knutsford, a hamlet about seven kilometres from Kamloops, with his father, John Wilkes Booth. His being named for the man who assassinated Abraham Lincoln suggests an odd quality in the family.

George Booth was a throwback, a man who might have been more comfortable in Kamloops in 1862 than in 1962, happier alone in the woods than with people. He got by on a meagre welfare payment and his skills as a woodsman.

He was a crack shot—his father boasted his son could split a match at fifty metres—and a master at making his own way in the rolling hills around Kamloops. He had built a fortified log cabin he planned to use as a retreat from civilization.

And he was a loner, suspicious of strangers, anyone in authority and, especially, police officers.

Five years earlier, his father had Booth committed to Essondale, a mental institution outside Vancouver. George kept claiming someone was poisoning his morning coffee. It was unnerving.

The four months of noisy, crowded confinement were nightmarish for a young man who cherished solitude and the outdoors.

RCMP officers took Booth to the institution. His father lied and told him the police had wanted him committed.

Still, there was nothing to suggest trouble on June 18, a hot and sunny Monday, when Booth set out for town. He wanted to find out why his welfare payments were getting smaller and renew the licence for a .303-calibre rifle, his father said.

Neighbour Anthony Parrott didn't think anything was unusual. He saw Booth walking and gave him a ride into town. George looked terrible. He was dressed for the bush, in a dirty jacket and brown cotton pants and a red-and-black checked flannel shirt, his black, curly hair wild, as always. His rifle was tucked into a buckskin sheath.

But he always looked terrible, Parrott said, and he seemed in good spirits.

Parrott dropped him near the provincial government buildings on the edge of Kamloops' small downtown.

And then things began to go bad.

Around nine o'clock, two conservation officers, George Ferguson and Frank Richter, saw Booth leaving the provincial building with a rifle. He seemed edgy. Ferguson asked where he was going.

Booth pushed the rifle barrel against Ferguson's stomach. "Get the hell out of here or I kill you."

They did. The wardens retreated to their office and called the RCMP.

Kamloops was a plum posting for young RCMP officers. With about 10,000 people, it was a comfortable size. The Thompson River runs through the heart of the city, and the hills and lakes provide the kind of recreation popular with the active young men from small towns who joined the RCMP in those days.

In the detachment, officers were getting ready for the day shift. They were hoping for a quiet time. The Indian Days weekend, with rodeos, sporting events, food and—inevitably—some drunkenness and brawling, had kept members busy breaking up fights and taking in drunks.

Monday was the voting day for the federal election, so bars were closed. Things should be peaceful.

Cst. Joe Keck took the call from the game wardens. He and Cst. Gord Pederson were assigned to investigate.

Keck was twenty-five and had grown up on a family grain farm in southern Saskatchewan. He was already a father, with another child on the way. He was good-looking, with a slender face and warm smile and wavy hair that drew movie star comparisons.

Pederson, from Milk River, Alberta, was two years younger, and barely back from his honeymoon. He didn't know it, but his wife was already pregnant.

Donald Weisgerber was on his day off. He had stopped in the detachment to do a few chores before heading to the golf course to try out the new clubs his wife had given him for his twenty-third birthday.

He was in casual clothes, and unarmed. But the call sounded interesting. He hopped in the cruiser with his friends.

It wasn't hard to find Booth. He was pacing outside the Motor Vehicle Office. The visit to town had not gone well.

He saw the three Mounties, and he brandished his rifle, still in its sheath. Everyone was immediately on edge.

Booth walked away from the building, and the officers followed, calling on him to stop and drop the gun—instructions he ignored.

With each step, the three young Mounties were heading toward disaster.

Within two minutes, the little group had covered 200 metres. Booth had walked along a dirt road that led to a mostly dry creek and a grassy, arid coulee. He took the rifle from its cover and dropped the sheath. Weisgerber, in his golf clothes, followed closely enough to pick it up and urge Booth to come back and get it.

Instead, Booth scrambled across the dry creek bed and waved the officers away. He pointed his rifle at them and yelled at them to leave him alone.

It was a surreal moment. Seniors from a nearby residence watched the standoff.

An angry man with a history of mental illness, armed with a rifle, faced three young, inexperienced Mounties—one of them unarmed, and the other two with revolvers.

In movies, shootouts unfold with some order, some logic. In real life, they are chaotic, noisy, and deadly.

Booth headed for a rough timber bridge over the creek. From there, he had a chance to disappear into scrub brush on the rising coulee sides.

Pedersen tried to cut off the escape. He closed the distance to twenty-five metres, as Keck and Weisgerber moved closer to the bridge.

But Booth had an overwhelming advantage.

He raised his rifle and aimed at Pederson, an easy target for an expert marksmen with a .303. The first bullet ripped across his back, the second missed, and amazingly Pederson snapped off one shot before dying instantly from a third bullet to the head.

Weisgerber, unarmed, ran for his life and dived behind a gravel skid box at the side of the dirt road, protection at least for the moment.

Keck rushed the bridge and made it underneath. He was shielded from a direct shot from Booth, desperately hoping for a chance to bring him down.

Incredibly, Keck managed to shoot Booth in the stomach, and he fell, dropping his rifle.

Weisgerber saw his chance and bolted from his hiding place, unarmed, to try and get the gun. He didn't make it. Booth picked up the rifle and shot him three times in the chest.

Keck edged out from under the bridge to see if Booth was wounded, leaning a little farther because he was still wearing his RCMP-issue brown stetson.

Booth shot him in the head and walked into the steep, bush-covered hill.

Three Mounties were dead. And Booth was wondering how his simple trip to town to complain about his welfare payments had gone so wrong.

Back at the detachment, Staff Sgt. Bernard d'Easum started to wonder the same thing. The phone lines were buzzing with reports of the shootings, and he couldn't reach the three officers on the car radio.

Siren screaming, he rushed to the scene. Every officer in the division scrambled to take part in the manhunt. The detachment didn't have enough rifles, so officers stopped by their homes or borrowed rifles from civilians keen to help. A helicopter hunted from the sky and dogs scoured the hillsides.

Booth's reputation as a ghost in the bush was deserved.

But no one could escape the dragnet.

Cpl. Jack White had stopped at home to get his own hunting rifle and, with two other officers, driven up into the hills to outflank Booth.

For two hours, they crept slowly down the hills. Just before noon, Booth suddenly appeared, standing in front of them. Everyone dove for cover, squeezing behind trees, pressing into the dirt.

"He was so close I could hear the action of his rifle as he worked the bolt to reload it," White said. They exchanged shots. When Booth rolled onto his side to reload, White shot him in the head.

But the story doesn't end with the shooting.

Cst. Pedersen's wife, Betty, was working in her new job in a Scotiabank branch when she saw Carole Finch, another RCMP wife, go into the manager's office.

Betty was called to the manager's office minutes later.

You need to come with me, Finch said. Gordon had "received an injury." But a bulletin on the car radio said there had been shooting and officers were dead. After a month of marriage, Pederson knew she was a widow.

Joan Weisgerber, working at her switchboard in the British Columbia Telephone building, was told by a supervisor there had been a "very bad accident" and Donald was dead.

And poor Ann Keck, pregnant with her second child, strolled into the RCMP detachment to remind Joe to vote before the end of the day. An officer had to tell her that Joe was dead.

More than 1,500 people attended the joint funeral service at the Kamloops arena. Thousands more lined the streets for the procession. Three flag-draped coffins.

John Wilkes Booth said the Mounties should have just let his boy walk away. He created a shrine in his tiny house, with George's blood-stained clothing on the wall. Built a concrete memorial on a mountaintop.

It was vandalized as fast as he could clean it up.

KIDNAPPED

S hayne Mulvahill was no one's idea of a criminal master-mind. He was definitely not a likely candidate to orches-trate the kidnapping of the daughter of Jimmy Pattison, one of Canada's richest men.

He had a tough childhood. His parents abused him, and he bounced through a series of foster homes. His behaviour landed him in a mental hospital for a year as a thirteen-year-old. A poor student, he made it through grade twelve in 1988 and headed straight into a series of unskilled jobs.

When he discovered that crime paid better, Mulvahill took to it with more enthusiasm than success.

The low point came in June 1989, when staff at a Vancouver McDonald's spotted him heading into the washroom at clos-ing time. They called police, who found Mulvahill weeping in a toilet stall. He had a loaded shotgun and a balaclava, but told officers he hadn't been able to decide whether to rob the place or kill himself.

By the beginning of 1990, Mulvahill was a twenty-year-old with no skills, big dreams, and a willingness to break the law. He just didn't know what crime to choose.

As winter turned to spring, Mulvahill and a friend spent afternoons in the Vancouver Public Library, where he read up on kidnappings. Easy money, he decided.

Once he had the crime, he began to research potential vic-tims, and Jimmy Pattison topped the list.

Not surprisingly. Pattison was a British Columbia legend. He started as a champion car salesman, talked his way into a loan to buy his own dealership, and motivated staff by firing the salesman who sold the fewest cars every month.

By 1990, he had built the largest private business in the province, capturing a major grocery chain, an airline, radio stations, and more. And the sixty-two-year-old Pattison had a big public profile, the man who made Expo 86 a success.

Mulvahill read Pattison's recent autobiography. He learned about Cynthia Kilburn, his thirty-year-old daughter, and found her address in a city directory in the library's reference section.

He worked on his plan. But Mulvahill was not good on details and had a problem with impulse control. His scheme was both bold and inept, a terrible combination. He didn't have a gang.

He pitched the idea to friend Jason Manchester, who said no.

So Manchester was surprised when Mulvahill asked him again, with a ransom note already typed. Manchester still said no, but, a week before the planned kidnapping, he introduced Mulvahill to nineteen-year-old Christian Snelgrove, a community college student with a full-time job and a stable family.

"I'm in," Snelgrove instantly said.

His job was to recruit three helpers to grab Cynthia Kilburn and hold her until the ransom was paid. He asked Nanami Kataoka to recruit the kidnappers from gang kids in North Vancouver, toughish teens with no real criminal experience.

Within days they were ready. A twenty-year-old mastermind. A nineteen-year-old second-in-command. Two armed teens—sixteen and seventeen—to do the kidnapping. A sixteen-year-old in charge of holding the hostage. No real plan.

It seemed more like the plot for a comedy movie than a serious crime.

But there was nothing funny about it for Cynthia Kilburn. Kilburn, her four-year-old twins, and the entire family were all about to face fourteen hours of terror.

Kilburn and her husband, Allan, lived a normal life, despite the family wealth, in a quiet North Vancouver neighbourhood. Neighbours had no idea she was rich enough to be a potential kidnap target.

Until December 21, 1990. Vancouver was suffering through a record cold snap, and Kilburn was fighting an illness, hoping to be better for a family Christmas. She had stayed in bed in the morning gloom, resting while keeping an ear out for her four-year-old twins, a boy and a girl.

The boy first noticed the two strangers coming up the front walk.

Kilburn answered the door. As soon as she saw the two young men standing there, clothes arranged to hide their faces, she tried to slam it closed.

But they pushed in, brandishing handguns. Kilburn was knocked down. The second man in pointed his gun at her and told her to co-operate or be shot. They bound her with tape, hands behind her back, ankles together, mouth and eyes covered. She struggled to breathe.

She heard her daughter calling for daddy. Then the children were dragged to an upstairs bathroom, bound hand and foot, and left alone. The phones were left off the hook.

The kidnappers dragged Kilburn to a stolen car, leaving a ransom note stuck to the front door. They wanted $200,000 right away, and $8.5 million for her return.

"If you call the police, she dies. If any media reports, she dies. Any slowdown in delivering the money, she dies. She is buried seven feet down in a wooden crate. She has three days' supply of bread and water."

The two kidnappers delivered Kilburn, still bound and blindfolded, to the sixteen-year-old accomplice. Kilburn struggled to breathe in the darkness, fearing she would die in the car.

The sixteen-year-old, not knowing what else to do, drove her to Manchester's parents' house, where he lived with his mom and dad.

Manchester had never agreed to be part of the kidnapping. He let them in, half-dragging Kilburn, who was bound and wrapped in a sleeping bag. But he was furious, calling Mulvahill and demanding to know "What the hell is going on."

Mulvahill and Snelgrove came and moved Kilburn—"the bundle," they called her—to the basement of another North Vancouver house.

By then, Kilburn's mother, Mary Pattison, had grown concerned because she couldn't reach her daughter. She sent an employee to check the house. The note was discovered on the door.

And things began to move quickly, strangely—and terrifyingly.

The Pattison family called police and gathered together. They feared Cynthia was buried alive. Jimmy Pattison arranged to get $200,000 from his bank.

Meanwhile, Mulvahill made calls to Pattison's direct line, Allan Kilburn's office, then his cellphone. He said the gang had Cynthia Kilburn, and threatened to kill her unless his instructions were followed. Around 8:15 p.m., he called Allan Kilburn's cellphone—the calls now being recorded by police—and gave instructions for the drop of the first $200,000.

The ransom drop is critical, the chance for police to grab the kidnapper and find out where the victim is being held.

Mulvahill told Kilburn to put the money in a red sports bag and take it to a specific entrance in the giant Hudson's Bay store downtown. There would be a note under a red tablecloth just inside the door, Mulvahill said. Kilburn had thirty seconds to follow the instructions and drop off the money.

It worked. Kilburn left the bag under a table, as the note demanded. Mulvahill watched him leave, stuffed the red bag full of money in a backpack, and ran into the attached mall.

Mulvahill imagined plainclothes police everywhere in the crowds of Christmas shoppers. He ducked into a washroom, then the posh Four Seasons Hotel. He called Kilburn repeatedly, telling him to call the police off or else.

In fact, police staking out the drop had already lost Mulvahill.

In North Vancouver, Snelgrove and Kataoka, watching Kilburn, were getting edgy because they hadn't heard from Mulvahill. The pair became convinced they had been double-crossed.

So they decided to let Cynthia Kilburn go, alternately apologizing to her and threatening and making excuses. Kataoka told her the original plan had been to take her on a plane and administer a heroin overdose.

The two teens argued about where to drop Kilburn, and then agreed to leave her near one of her friends' houses in North Vancouver. The van stopped, and Kilburn had one more moment of terror as she waited to be shot. Instead, Snelgrove apologized and said he got greedy. Kataoka walked her a short distance, then told her to run.

Barefoot, still in the housecoat she was wearing fourteen hours earlier, Kilburn clawed the tape from her eyes and ran toward the front door of her friend's house.

The prospects of an $8.5 million total ransom vanished.

But incredibly, a band of hapless amateurs had scored $200,000, and got away with it.

Not for long though. There is a sequence in the mob movie *Goodfellas* in which Robert De Niro kills his accomplices in a big heist because they ignore his order not to go out and show off their new money.

Mulvahill, Snelgrove, and the rest—together happily, despite their earlier rifts—must not have seen the movie. On Saturday, they hired a white stretch limousine and headed out to spend some of their newfound wealth.

Amazingly, they made the downtown Hudson's Bay store one of their first stops. Security staff had all been given a description of Mulvahill based on the police surveillance when he picked up the ransom. An alert guard did a double take when he saw Mulvahill, then called police with a description of the limo.

Every officer in the city was told to watch for the limo and the gang. And soon police saw the car heading into a shopping centre in West Vancouver.

Mulvahill was arrested as he took seven new suits in to a tailor for alterations. The limo driver said they had visited four shopping centres, and the gang had filled the roomy trunk with clothes, jewelry, and guitars, handing $1,000 to a panhandler at one stop.

* * *

Seven people were arrested that day—all five people directly involved and a couple of hangers-on charged with possession of stolen property.

Mulvahill and Snelgrove faced the most serious charges—kidnapping, extortion, and confinement of Kilburn's twin children. They pleaded not guilty, but two days into the trial, admitted their guilt.

Mulvahill got life for kidnapping and extortion, and seven years for confining the children. Snelgrove was sentenced to thirteen years for each of the kidnapping and extortion charges, and seven years for his role in the twins' confinement. Both appealed, and Mulvahill's life terms were reduced to eighteen years and Snelgrove's sentences reduced from thirteen to ten years. The others, judged minor players, got shorter sentences.

For the Kilburns and the Pattisons, everything changed. Vancouver was no longer such a safe place. A knock on the door could bring a wave of terror.

Jimmy Pattison said the family now worried any time someone was late for a gathering, or didn't answer the phone. "We are constantly looking over our shoulders for suspicious cars, people and circumstances." The family introduced security measures they had never considered necessary. Vancouver changed a little, for the worse.

The criminals were dim-witted bunglers, said British Columbia Supreme Court Justice Ken Meredith during sentencing. Their plan was laughable.

But that problem made them more dangerous, he said. "The more harebrained the scheme the greater the risk to life."

POSTSCRIPT

The penitentiary system is supposed to make people "penitent" and ready to live better lives.

It didn't work for the kidnappers.

Naname Kataoka served three years for his role in the kidnapping. Once released, he renewed his gang ties, linking up with the feared United Nations gang. In 2009, he was found shot to death in a parking lot in Buenos Aires.

Christian Snelgrove served a little more than three years, and at first did well on release. But heroin, then crack, called him, and in 2003 he broke into his ex-common-law partner's home, threatened her and their baby, and forced them into his car. He was sent back to prison for four years.

And Shayne Mulvahill turned into the poster boy for the failure of the penal system. He was released on day parole in 1998. But he had heard jailhouse gossip about a convicted cocaine dealer who was about to come into some big money. So Mulvahill hatched a plan to kidnap the man's adult son. It all went wrong, the victim escaped, and Mulahill was sent back to jail with another twenty-year sentence.

Jimmy Pattison's success continued. In 2013, he was Canada's richest man. But he still lost something that money couldn't buy on that day before Christmas in 1990.

HOCKEY ON TRIAL

Boston Bruin Marty McSorley's crime lasted only seconds. It took place under bright white TV lights, in front of 14,000 eyewitnesses, and left Vancouver Canuck Donald Brashear unconscious and convulsing on the ice in Vancouver's GM Place.

And, at least briefly, it sparked a critical look at hockey's unwritten code of violence and intimidation.

McSorley had already earned millions of dollars fighting other hockey players by the time he squared off against Brashear on February 21, 2000.

From his first days with junior hockey Belleville Bulls, McSorley understood his role. When hockey's code—or a coach—said it was time to fight, he jumped over the boards, dropped his gloves, and started punching.

His willingness—and fearsomeness—carried him to the NHL. Without his ability to fight, McSorley acknowledged, he never would have even made a Junior A team, the first rung on the long ladder to the top.

But an enforcer's career is tenuous. Younger, stronger, fiercer players are always arriving. Like gunslingers in the Wild West, they know that beating the best is the way to make their mark—and the big money.

By the 1999 season, McSorley's career was waning. The year before, for the first time, he had lost more fights than he had won. He was thirty-six—old in a trade that requires you to absorb hundreds of punches to the head and square off in brawls with other men, facing not just physical punishment but humiliation in front of thousands of people who cheer as you are battered.

McSorley had been released by his last two teams before he signed with the Boston Bruins that year. His annual salary, almost $2 million in 1995, had fallen to around $600,000. His glory years as Wayne Gretzky's on-ice bodyguard in Edmonton and Los Angeles and his two Stanley Cup wins were in the past.

McSorley had worked to become a more complete hockey player. He was a respected representative in the players' association. His flowing golden hair and good looks made him a fan favourite.

But he was paid to be a tough guy, and after 274 NHL fights, McSorley still had something to prove.

Brashear's career was going the other way. He had only made it as a full-time NHL player four years earlier with the Montreal Canadiens, but his salary had already climbed from $170,000 to $750,000. He was feared, and the future looked bright as long as he kept on winning fights.

It wasn't surprising Brashear was a fighter. His childhood was grim. He was born in Indiana, with an African-American father and a mother from Quebec. He was abused and beaten, abandoned for a time by his mother, and ended up in foster care in Quebec. He discovered hockey, and sold bread and garbage bags door-to-door and delivered papers to cover the costs. The toughest NHL bad man wasn't likely to scare him after his real-life battles.

* * *

The Bruins and Canucks were both struggling to make the playoffs when they played on February 21.

McSorley thought his team seemed listless, and needed a spark. Two minutes into the game, he decided to provoke a fight with Brashear, the Canucks' enforcer. That was part of his job.

McSorley cross-checked Brashear from behind, a challenge. The two threw off their gloves and started fighting.

Brashear—twelve years younger and bigger—won, finishing with a powerful body punch that left McSorley in obvious pain and then tossing him to the ice. The Canucks' fans loved it.

Enforcers know they'll lose fights. They trade punches with other big, strong, and skilled brawlers, whose livelihoods depend on their ability to inflict pain.

But losers have to show they aren't intimidated. That they still are the intimidator, still ready to battle.

After the fight, Brashear broke one of the rules in hockey's mysterious, unwritten code of conduct, skating past the Boston bench and dusting off his hands as Canucks' fans cheered. Showing up your fellow combatant is bad.

So McSorley had at least two reasons for wanting a rematch. Ten minutes later, he cross-checked Brashear, knocking him to the ice, then shoved at him several times, grabbed his sweater, and refused to back off when the linesman intervened and the fans screamed for action.

"Come on, Don, you have to fight me again," McSorley challenged.

"No Marty, I'm not going to fight you," Brashear said. "We're beating you four-nothing." (The first-name friendliness is a reminder that hockey violence, particularly between enforcers, is usually just business.)

McSorley's attempt hurt his team, as he received a pair of two-minute penalties and a ten-minute misconduct. While he was off the ice, Brashear fell on Bruins goalie Byron Dafoe during a melee, and Dafoe left the game clutching his knee. Another violation of the code.

Later, after another Bruin was penalized for slashing Brashear, he taunted the Bruins again, striking a muscleman pose on the bench.

With a minute to go, the Bruins were ahead five to two. McSorley was sitting on the bench, waiting for the buzzer.

But with about twenty seconds left, Boston assistant coach Jacques Laperriere ordered him on the ice.

The order was clear, McSorley said. Fight Brashear again. (Laperriere was not known as a fighter in his long career with the Montreal Canadiens, and quit his first coaching job in junior hockey because of the goon tactics dominating the Quebec league.)

Brashear didn't want to fight, and actively avoided McSorley.

McSorley wanted to do his job, and maybe boost his team's confidence. Time was running out. So he decided to slash Brashear to provoke an unavoidable confrontation.

With three seconds left, he hit Brashear in the side of the head with a two-handed swing. The Canuck's helmet flew off, and he fell unconscious to the ice, striking his head. He lay unconscious, legs splayed, eyes open, experiencing a seizure as fans booed and threw trash, trainers rushed to his aid, and the players on the ice brawled. The concussion kept him from any physical activity for a month.

The fight was over on the ice. Off the ice, it was just beginning.

The NHL always argued that hockey existed in a separate world and criminal laws should not apply. The leagues would use suspensions or fines to keep order. Players would impose their own violent retribution on those who broke the unwritten code that defined acceptable and unacceptable violence. It had been twelve years since Minnesota's Dino Ciccarelli was sentenced to one day in jail and fined $1,000 for hitting Toronto defenceman Luke Richardson several times in the head with his stick.

Vancouver Canucks' general manager Brian Burke, even though his player Brashear could have been killed, said police should stay out of it. "Leave this stuff on the ice; leave it to the National Hockey League," he told a radio station. "We don't need the Vancouver police department or the RCMP involved in this."

CBC commentator Don Cherry said the head shot was wrong, but Brashear caused the problem by ridiculing McSorley. "If you want to play with a bull, you're going to get the horns."

McSorley quickly apologized and said he hadn't meant to hit Brashear in the head. "I embarrassed my hockey team," he said. "I got way too carried away. It was a real dumb play."

But the devastating video had been seen by millions, and the league suspended McSorley for a year, the longest suspension in its history.

Police and British Columbia Crown prosecutors didn't back off. And on September 26, McSorley walked into a Vancouver provincial court with his two lawyers to face a charge of assault with a weapon.

Both McSorley and the NHL's culture of violence were on trial.

Especially the unwritten code that, despite the official rules, sanctioned slashing and fighting and brawls in some circumstances.

McSorley's defence team advanced two arguments.

First, that slashing is accepted, under the unwritten code of conduct, as a way to start a fight. Brashear knew that, and thus implicitly consented to being hit with a hockey stick, even with a blow aimed inches from his head.

Second, that McSorley had swung his stick at Brashear's shoulder, not his head. His only offence was inaccuracy.

A parade of hockey celebrities testified. The referee, Brad Watson, and linesman Michael Cvik described their practice in enforcing both the rules and hockey's unwritten code.

Brashear was a sullen, monosyllabic witness. He acknowledged he did not consent to be hit in the head, but made it clear he didn't want to be in court and didn't think McSorley should be either.

And McSorley, with his friend Gretzky there to provide support, said he was sorry, but insisted he hadn't been angry and hadn't meant to hit "Donald" in the head. He was sent out to fight, Brashear was reluctant, and a two-handed slash to the shoulder was an accepted way to force the issue.

Judge Bill Kitchen called McSorley "bright and articulate" and "a likeable personality."

But he wasn't convinced McSorley had missed his target.

"He slashed for the head. A child, swinging as at a Tee ball, would not miss. A housekeeper swinging a carpet beater would not miss. An NHL player would never, ever miss. Brashear was struck as intended," Kitchen said. "Mr. McSorley, I must find you guilty as charged."

"Everyone must understand that this type of violence won't be tolerated, either on a street or in a hockey arena."

Hockey wasn't on trial, said Kitchen, a fan. But McSorley's slash to the head should prompt fans and players to consider the role of violence in the game.

"There is work to be done," he suggested. "The game deserves it."

McSorley never played in the NHL again, but worked as a minor-league coach, TV commentator, and sometimes actor, including a role on *CSI: Miami*.

Brashear played another nine seasons, fought 160 more times, and was paid another $12.8 million before his NHL career as an enforcer came to an end.

SEX ON-CAMERA

Poor Bob McLelland. The popular provincial cabinet minister was a little drunk when he picked up the phone in his Chateau Victoria hotel room and called Top Hat Productions.

The name suggested a film company. But Top Hat offered different, more specialized, entertainment.

McLelland asked if a "girl" could be sent to his room, how much it would cost, and—unfortunately—if he could pay with his Visa card.

Arlie Blakely, the forty-two-year-old mom who ran Top Hat, happily obliged.

Neither of them knew, on that February night in 1985, that Victoria police, RCMP, and prosecutors had launched an extraordinary effort to bust Blakely, with wiretaps, surveillance, and spy cameras pushing the boundaries of privacy laws.

McLelland's $130 tryst landed him in the middle of the mess. Even though he had broken no law, since paying for sex was, and is, legal in Canada.

McLelland was a terrifically popular Social Credit MLA from Langley. He had served thirteen years in the legislature and held some of the toughest cabinet portfolios. He even finished second in the 1973 party leadership race that crowned Bill Bennett as the successor to his father, the legendary W. A. C. Bennett.

Twice married, the father of two children, McLelland was handsome, with dark hair, tanned skin, and an easy smile. His resonant voice betrayed his past work as a radio announcer.

He had style and liked to have fun. For the Socred's giant final rally for the 1975 election campaign, McLelland entered the Vancouver arena riding an elephant named Tina, despite party honchos' fears of the havoc an out-of-control elephant could wreak on the crowd of supporters.

After his night with the escort, McLelland headed off the next morning—February 27—to Government House, where he was sworn into a new cabinet post by the lieutenant-governor.

He had no idea that everyone would soon be talking about his night of paid sex.

* * *

On May 6, Crown prosecutors charged Blakely with nineteen prostitution-related offences—procuring illicit sex, aiding and abetting, and living off the avails of prostitution. While prostitution itself was and is legal, all the activities around it are against the law.

She went out the next day and hired a feisty young lawyer, Robert Moore-Stewart.

As the charges hit the news, rumours about the huge police operation and high-profile clients started sweeping through the city. Victoria was a company town, and government was the company. Politicians and government employees made up a large part of the population. Gossip travelled fast.

Moore-Stewart planned to use the most obvious defence.

Blakely was just arranging appointments, he would argue. She didn't know what McLelland and the other clients got for their $130. She was simply answering the phone and arranging meetings.

When he learned police had found Bob McLelland's Visa slip in the Top Hat files, Moore-Stewart saw an opportunity.

He talked to Blakely and the escort who had sex with McLelland, and decided the cabinet minister could be a helpful defence witness.

McLelland could testify that sex was never discussed with Blakely, supporting the argument that she was just arranging a meeting. The rest was up to the escort and the client.

And it almost certainly crossed Moore-Stewart's mind that Crown prosecutors might be a little reluctant to pursue a case if a cabinet minister was going to be embarrassed on the witness stand.

Meanwhile, the buzz of rumours about high-profile clients was becoming a roar, with lightly veiled references to politicians paying for Top Hat sex in a popular newspaper column. Tales of a list of prominent clients and special protection for the powerful by police and prosecutors spread through the city.

Reporters called Moore-Stewart throughout that summer, sharing what they had heard and pumping him for information. Prosecutors and police spokesmen and politicians stuck to a terse no-comment policy.

Moore-Stewart heard another cabinet minister, Terry Segarty, had been with McLelland earlier that evening.

He decided to go before a justice of the peace and obtain subpoenas to call Segarty and McLelland as defence witnesses at the November trial.

He had to move quickly. MLAs could ignore subpoenas served less than forty days before a scheduled legislative sitting, and the Socreds had announced a fall session. (The law was intended to prevent unscrupulous political parties from using subpoenas to deplete the ranks of their opponents. It was a legitimate concern in the days when travel by horse or coach could take days, but an anachronism in 1985.)

The justice of the peace accepted Moore-Stewart's statement that he believed the two ministers might have useful information and issued the warrants.

But the case was sensitive. No leaks, he warned courthouse staff. Absolutely none.

He got home that evening, turned on the TV, and saw that the subpoenas were already big, big news. Moore-Stewart was the most likely source.

It was an intriguing tactic, if Moore-Stewart was behind the leak. Send the message that the trial wouldn't just focus on Arlie Blakely's escort business. The clients, perhaps police and prosecutors, could all face unwelcome attention and uncomfortable questions.

And there were uncomfortable questions. The police had spent $50,000 on the investigation. They had drilled holes through motel walls and, without a search warrant, videotaped hours of activity—sex—in the next room.

Officers spent eight weeks capturing wiretap recordings and videos and keeping up a massive surveillance effort. They threatened clients—testify against Blakely, or the videos of your paid sex will be shown in court.

And they had singled out Top Hat, even though there were a half-dozen escort agencies advertising in the Yellow Pages and Victoria newspapers.

All to charge one mom with minor offences.

And the prosecutors, despite eight weeks of surveillance, chose to lay charges relating to one week—February 14 to February 21. The time frame excluded McLelland's order for a "girl." Why so few charges, people wondered in the coffee shops and at the cocktail parties, and why pick that one week? Who were the clients in the other seven weeks of surveillance?

The pressure on Moore-Stewart and Blakely was fierce.

McLelland hired a high-profile lawyer, who told Moore-Stewart—wrongly, as it turned out—that McLelland's testimony would be damaging to Blakely. (Segarty's subpoena was quashed, as he had only breakfasted with McLelland that morning, long before the Top Hat call. He was unfairly maligned by Moore-Stewart.)

And the attention on the trial was just as intense. TV camera crews and news photographers staked out the courthouse steps.

Blakely hardly looked the part of a madam or pimp. She was a strapping woman with short, brown, permed hair and a friendly smile, little or no makeup, dressed more like a suburban mom many days, in red fleece jacket, dark slacks, and white shirt.

Moore-Stewart did his best to put the police and prosecutors on trial.

A police officer faced tough questions about the decision to rent a motel room next to one occupied by an escort, drill a hole in the wall, and set up a video camera. When wiretaps indicated a client visit was scheduled, the police started filming.

The senior officer testified it was a first for him, but prosecutors told him no search warrant was needed—as long as the sound was turned off. Prosecutors exploited a loophole in the law, which didn't contemplate cheap and easy video spying.

McLelland's day in court came on November 27, a snowy Wednesday. He arrived alone, collar turned up on his black coat, looking, one reporter noted, "glum." How else would a married politician look on the way into court to admit hiring a prostitute?

McLelland said he made the call to Top Hat and asked for a woman. "I'd had a fair amount of drink that evening," he testified. "I would say it would have been late."

Moore-Stewart tried to ask more questions about the encounter, the Crown objected, and—because McLelland bought sex outside the one-week window specified by the prosecutors—the judge would not allow the questions.

But McLelland did confirm he had never discussed sex or what he expected when he arranged the $130-an-hour encounter in the phone call with Blakely.

Then he walked back to the legislature through the snow, refusing to answer questions from the pack of reporters.

Embarrassing, even humiliating, especially as the Socreds claimed the moral high ground. But Premier Bill Bennett, while agreeing McLelland had hardly set a good example, didn't drop him from cabinet. His fellow MLAs and Langley politicians also supported him.

"I don't think it's my business to poke into other people's business, particularly gossipy, junky stuff," said Cliff Michael, chair of the Socred caucus.

Which, implicitly, raised questions about what the RCMP, Victoria police, and Crown prosecutors were doing poking into the business of Top Hat, the women who worked there, and the men who paid for services.

The trial ended. The jury—five men, seven women—found Blakely guilty of ten counts.

But Judge Robert Hutchison—ex-Olympic athlete, son of pre-eminent British Columbia journalist and writer Bruce Hutchison—imposed a token penalty. Blakely was sentenced to the one day in jail she had already served, a $900 fine, six months' probation, and community service.

When society is willing to let people pay for sex with credit cards, he asked, can we really say we consider prostitution a serious offence?

McLelland didn't run in the next election. Segarty did, lost, and blamed the unfair bad publicity from the trial.

Blakely paid her fine and did community service.

At least one of the sex workers attempted suicide when she learned lawyers wanted to use her name in court.

Police and prosecutors faced tough questions about the costly investigation and the dubious secret videotapes. The provincial government ordered an inquiry and called for controls on police spying without warrants.

Moore-Stewart paid the highest price. He went too far in getting the subpoena for Segarty, but he also successfully put the system on trial and exposed the legal hypocrisy that saw McLelland go uncharged while Blakely faced jail time for answering the phone.

But his aggressive tactics got him into trouble with the Law Society of British Columbia, which regulates lawyers. After a legal battle that he took up all the way up to the British Columbia Court of Appeal, Moore-Stewart ended up paying a fine and went on to a career of representing outsider clients.

And escort agencies kept on fielding late-night calls from customers in upscale hotels.

GENTLEMAN OUTLAW

Bill Miner rode across the Canadian border in the fall of 1903, one step ahead of the Pinkerton men and the police, a price on his head.

He was fifty-six. Old for an outlaw. San Quentin prison was the closest thing he ever had to a home. Robbing was his only real trade.

The hard life was etched on his face. A bushy white moustache almost covered his wide mouth, beneath a long nose and penetrating dark eyes. Usually, a wide-brimmed stetson hid his swept-back hair. He looked tired.

The wanted posters put him at five foot nine and about 145 pounds, and noted the tattooed dancing girl on his right forearm.

Miner, the gentleman bandit, was on the run again. And he was on the way to becoming a Canadian legend.

* * *

Miner lied the way other men breathed, so it's hard to separate myth from reality. He was born in Michigan, and his family moved to a California gold town after his father died.

Miner signed on with the California Cavalry Volunteers in 1864, on the side of the north in the bloody Civil War. He deserted after three months.

And he took to crime. It was a good time to be a criminal in the West. Lawmen were few and communication was slow. A robber could take what he wanted and be in any other county, using a different name, before the victim found a sheriff.

Miner had style. At nineteen, he rode to a nearby town on a stolen horse, picked out a fine suit, and asked the clerk to come with him while he fetched the money to pay for it. Once in an alley, Miner pulled a pistol and told the clerk he was taking the suit, and his watch. Stand there for twenty minutes, and everything would be fine, he said. The clerk, "overpowered by the robber's chivalrous bearing ... stood there shivering ... until the 20 minutes had expired," reported the local paper.

His life of crime was under way. He stole money and horses, and eventually tried a stagecoach robbery with an accomplice.

But they were tracked and caught, sleeping in a hotel room. It was one of a long series of captures.

Still nineteen, Miner started his first stretch in San Quentin, treating the sentence as an inconvenience at worst, a badge of honour at best.

San Quentin was grim and violent, a three-storey stone building with two inmates sharing each four-foot-by-nine-foot cell. Prisoners were whipped and tortured for breaking the rules.

It should have been a powerful deterrent. But as soon as Miner was free, he went back to stealing. And didn't get much better at it.

Miner teamed up with "Alkali Jim" Harrington, a contact from San Quentin, on a string of burglaries and, with an accomplice named Charlie Cooper, a stagecoach robbery that earned them some $2,600 in gold. But Harrington and Miner betrayed Cooper, taking off with the money. When Cooper was caught, he was quick to implicate them.

Miner and Harrington dodged capture in one shootout with police in San Jose. It wan't like the movies. The outlaws' guns didn't work, they ran away, and no one on either side got hurt.

But the law caught up with Miner in San Francisco in February 1871. He was sent back to San Quentin for another nine years.

When he got out, Miner was thirty-three. He was likeable and polite, and his letters seeking early release are articulate and persuasive. He had been a criminal for about fifteen years, and spent thirteen of them behind bars. Another man might have decided on a career change.

But Miner went right back to robbing, heading to southern Colorado and hooking up with a new, older partner who called himself Billy LeRoy. They robbed at least three stagecoaches in 1880—without violence—finally hitting a $4,000 jackpot.

Miner headed east with his share. LeRoy, with his brother, kept on robbing, until they were lynched a year later by the "People's Committee for Safety" in Del Norte, Colorado.

Miner's eastern break was short. By the spring of 1881, he was back in the West, staging robberies and thefts in Colorado and California. He was more skilful, and the legend of the gentleman bandit grew. Newspapers reported his courteous banter with the coach drivers and passengers. A wanted poster described a charming, fashionable felon—"a good fluent talker, fond of women," who had spent $85 of the loot on black beaver pants, a "silk plush vest, quite flashy," and a dark chinchilla coat.

He didn't get to wear them long. On December 7, 1881, Miner was captured by a Wells Fargo detective. Ten days later, he was on his way back to San Quentin. It was an eventful stay—he was shot and wounded in an escape attempt, stabbed by another inmate, and pleaded his case for release.

In 1901, Miner once again walked through the prison gate a free man. He was older—fifty-four—but not much wiser despite twenty-three years in prison.

The West had changed while Miner was behind bars. Law and order had come to the frontier. Stagecoaches had been replaced by trains. Telephones linked communities.

Miner headed to northwest Washington State, and stayed out of trouble for a time. But on September 23, 1903, Miner was part of a dynamite-waving gang that botched a train robbery outside Portland, Oregon. Within days, a $1,300 reward was being offered by the railway and the state.

It was time to head to Canada. Miner laid low around Princeton for a while, winning friends in the community. He hooked up with another San Quentin alumnus, "Cowboy" Jack Terry, and helped him in his smuggling business. Opium was legal in Canada until 1908, but banned in the United States. Then, as now, there was money in the drug trade.

But less than a year after the Portland debacle, Miner decided to go back to robbing trains. This time, he got it right.

Miner and two accomplices travelled to Mission Junction and waited for the Vancouver-bound Canadian Pacific Railway train No. 1 on September 10, 1904. It was a foggy night; they had no trouble dropping from the water tower onto the baggage car during the train's brief stop.

Wearing masks and brandishing revolvers and a rifle, they made their way to the engine as the train pulled away and ordered the driver to stop just down the line. The raid on the express car was a huge success—some $6,000 in gold dust, $900 in cash, and $50,000 in United States bonds.

It wasn't just a big score. Miner's gang is credited with the first train robbery in Canada, and he—perhaps apocryphally—was said to have used the phrase "Hands up" for the first time in a heist.

The robbery could have paid for a nice retirement. Miner had friends at Princeton and was liked in the community, stepping in to help neighbours when needed. There was ranch work if he wanted it. He was fifty-seven.

But Miner had other plans. On May 8, 1906, he and two others clambered onto a westbound CPR express while it was stopped to take on water at Ducks, just outside Kamloops. The engineer soon found himself "staring down the barrel of a big revolver."

The robbery was a fiasco. Miner told the engineer to stop the train, and the engine and mail car were disconnected and run a mile down the track. Unfortunately, the express car, most likely to hold valuables, was left behind. The robbers came up with almost nothing and, worse, missed packages containing about $40,000 in cash and gold.

Miner's age was showing. The *British Colonist* reported, "An old man was evidently in command of the robbery." It was the same gang responsible for the 1904 train robbery, the paper reported.

"The mask fell off the old man's face ... and Mail Clerk Thorburn, who was in the former hold-up, recognized him."

It was Bill Miner, the paper said. And he maintained his trademark politeness. When he noticed one of the train staff was shivering, he apologized, adding "we won't keep you long."

This time, the CPR wasn't going to let Miner get away. An $11,500 reward was quickly posted by the railway, Canada, and the province.

The money would be paid for any one of the robbers—"Dead or Alive."

About 100 people set out from Kamloops to try to claim the reward. Fortunately for the outlaws, a team of Royal Northwest Mounted Police officers found them first. Shorty Dunn, one of the gang, fired on the officers and was wounded, but the three were ultimately taken into custody peacefully.

On June 1, 1906, Miner was sent to prison again—this time for life.

It didn't work out that way. A little over a year later, Miner escaped from the New Westminster Penitentiary. (There has been speculation that his escape was arranged, part of a deal to return the $50,000 in bonds stolen in 1904 to the CPR.)

By then, the legend was as big as the man. Miner had public sympathy. "Bill Miner's not so bad," a joke went. "He only robs the CPR every two years, they rob us every day."

The *Colonist* reported that citizens around Princeton cheered his getaway. "He is spoken of by all who knew him as a most amiable, open-hearted, kindly old fellow ... who would go out of his way to do a good turn to his fellow man," the paper said. "He is regarded as a Robin Hood of these later days of steam railways."

Miner wasn't done yet. He made his way to Georgia, and in 1911, at sixty-five, robbed the Southern Railway express. Caught and sent to prison, he escaped twice more. He was captured quickly each time, but the legend grew. The newspapers compared him to Jesse James, celebrated his wit and cunning and courtesy, called him the last of the Western outlaws.

On Sept. 2, 1913, Bill Miner died in prison at sixty-seven.

His legend lives on.

WAITING DEMONS

Stephen Reid was an outlaw and legend, like Bill Miner. Only a century later.

Miner robbed trains and stagecoaches. Reid robbed banks. A lot of banks.

But Reid, it seemed, left that world. He met the love of his life, a brilliant poet, while he was serving a long prison term. He wrote a fine and successful novel behind bars.

Once he'd done his time, Reid settled into life with his wife and two beautiful daughters in a little house with a tree growing up through the roof, on a saltwater inlet near Victoria. He was a success, a great teacher and fine writer. Funny, wise, calm—someone people wanted to be around.

It was a perfect story. Until one day in June 1999, when it wasn't.

* * *

There is a blurry line between legend and lie.

Stephen Reid's legend had him born in 1950 in Massey, a small Ontario town on the northern shores of Georgian Bay. He was bright, good-looking, an athlete, second of eight children in a solidly middle-class home.

Until suddenly, at sixteen, he decided to hitchhike to Vancouver for the summer, where he was caught with half a joint and tangled up in the courts. He got back too late for high school that year, worked in the mine where his father was the office manager, but didn't much like mining. Ended up in Toronto using hard drugs and robbing, first corner stores and then banks. Jailed at twenty-two, he escaped by persuading two guards accompanying him on a day pass to stop for Chinese food and disappearing out the washroom window. Made his way to Ottawa, and met charming crime kingpin Paddy Mitchell.

Read it quickly and it almost makes sense. But the legend leaves out some parts of the story. Dark parts, things harder to leave behind than the thrill of robbing banks.

Reid did meet Paddy Mitchell, a charismatic and creative crook who had the ability to find good scores and bring the right people together to make them happen.

Mitchell was ten years older, a family man, wildly social. But he and Reid, big moustaches and bigger smiles, were an amazing team. Especially when they hooked up with Lionel Wright, the introverted, thoughtful loner who could plan any crime down to the last detail.

Their first crime together was an April 1974 robbery that saw them walk away with $700,000 worth of gold from a poorly guarded Air Canada freight storage building at the Ottawa airport. It was the kind of score that makes crime seem a very good career choice.

Reid hardly had time to enjoy the money. He was still a wanted man after his Chinese restaurant escape. In December, police grabbed him and he was sent back to jail after fourteen months on the street.

Wright and Mitchell joined Reid behind bars a little more than a year later, locked up on drug trafficking conspiracy charges.

But the trio didn't stick around for long. Wright escaped within months. It took Reid longer, but in August 1979, he persuaded another guard accompanying him on a day pass to let him have a forbidden meal, fish and chips this time. Once again, he said he was going to the restaurant washroom and never came back.

Three months later, Mitchell steeped cigarette tobacco in water to brew a nicotine broth in his cell. He drank it, went for a run in the prison yard, and collapsed with the symptoms of a heart attack. The prison rushed him by ambulance to the nearest hospital. Wright and Reid were waiting. They directed it to a side entrance, pulled guns on the attendants, and carried Mitchell away.

The trio fled to Florida, and then California and the West. And they started getting serious about robberies.

Reid and Wright studied the target banks and department stores, the local police patrols, escape routes, and when there was likely to be the most money. They stole getaway cars and used elaborate disguises to distract witnesses, like Richard Nixon masks or dramatic makeup jobs. Wright even tracked garbage pickup schedules and made sure to get rid of evidence just before a truck was due to empty the Dumpsters.

And Reid wore a stopwatch around his neck, a reminder to stay in the bank less than ninety seconds. They became the Stopwatch Gang, high on the FBI's Most Wanted list.

It worked for a while. Reid, Mitchell, and Wright were armed robbery champions, flush with cash, living the high life. They had a hideaway in Sedona, Arizona, amid the stunning red rock towers and the vortexes of spiritual energy that attracted New Age seekers.

But less than two years after they began their U.S. crime wave, the FBI busted Reid and Wright in Sedona in October 1981.

They had made crime pay and stolen millions. And, as much through good luck as good management, they had never shot anyone.

Reid was sentenced to ten years on December 15, 1981, and sent back to a Canadian penitentiary—Millhaven Institute, a violent maximum-security prison—in May 1983. He started writing a novel based on his life in crime, which made its way to poet Susan Musgrave, the writer-in-residence at the University of Waterloo.

She liked the writing; they fell in love and were married inside a maximum security prison outside Vancouver in 1986. Reid's novel, *Jackrabbit Parole*, came out the same year and to great reviews.

A year later, Reid was paroled.

It should have been the best of all possible times. Reid was only thirty-six. He was charming, amusing, calming, a brilliant writing instructor and a powerful and witty writer, an effective advocate for prisoners, a champion of restorative justice.

Musgrave was, he says, "one of the most beautiful and interesting women on the planet." Their children—her daughter from a previous marriage, Charlotte, and the daughter they had together, Sophie—were "two incredible pieces of magic." He was sought after, embraced by the writing community (though maybe trapped too much in the role of outlaw).

* * *

But it wasn't enough. All that light couldn't penetrate the dark places.

That legend of the young man who went from athlete and student to bank robber in barely a teenage summer left out a chapter. It left out Dr. Paul, the pedophile who introduced Reid to morphine and money and sex and betrayal when he was just eleven.

It left out the dance with the drugs that were always waiting for their time to come again.

In the spring of 1999, the drugs were calling. Reid answered.

And within three months, everything had gone wrong. He owed $90,000 for a stupid, botched cocaine deal, with no way to pay. The bill was due, and the people who fronted the cash didn't like excuses.

So on June 9, Reid, in a heroin haze, set out to rob a bank in Victoria's Cook Street Village, a stretch of cute coffee shops and markets a few blocks from the ocean.

It was, Reid says, a crime against crime. No planning. A getaway driver he calls Lintball, a mask that made him look like "bank-robber Barbie," and four guns, including a Chinese assault rifle. Too long in the bank, no escape route, midmorning traffic.

By the time he left the bank, police were waiting. There was a stupid, dangerous attempt to escape, hanging out the car window, firing at the pursuing police with a shotgun. Pushing into an apartment with two frightened seniors. Falling asleep on a couch while the police waited to come in.

And, after twelve years, back to the penitentiary, this time on an eighteen-year sentence.

Reid wrote an award-winning book of essays, *A Crowbar in the Buddhist Garden*, during this prison term. He served nine years while his daughters grew up, got out on day parole, and was caught with 3,600 contraband cigarettes while driving without a licence. He was sent back to prison.

He was released on day parole again in 2014, a grandfather. Determined, he says, to fall toward grace this time.

THOSE McLEAN BOYS

Maybe Johnny Ussher thought the Wild McLean boys—the youngest just fifteen—weren't real outlaws.

Or maybe it was foolish to think a Montreal-raised lawyer's son, an accidental constable in the Canadian West, could deal with the McLeans, products of a hard land and an even harder father.

But when Ussher rode out into the Kamloops country with three other men to arrest the McLean boys on a snowy day in December 1879, he made a fatal mistake.

The McLeans were not ones to go quietly.

While Frank and Jesse James roamed the American midwest, the McLean gang—brothers Allan, Charlie, and Archie, with their friend Alex Hare—were riding British Columbia's northern interior, taking what they wanted, daring any man to stop them, and growing bolder and more dangerous.

They were young. Allan was twenty-five when the gang killed Ussher. Charlie was seventeen, like Alex Hare. Archie was just fifteen.

But they rode the hills and grasslands around Kamloops and into the Cariboo like outlaw lords. If they were thirsty, they took your whiskey. If they liked your horse, they rode away with it. If they were hungry, or wanted guns, you did not want to get in their way.

It was Archie—fifteen and looking younger, with cropped hair and a boy's face, baggy pants held high on his waist with a rope, trying to look tough and win his brothers' respect—who put the bullet into Ussher's head.

The McLean boys were the sons of Donald McLean, a hard man even by the standards of the frontier.

McLean grew up on the Isle of Mull, a windy, wild island off Scotland's west coast. He set out at twenty-eight to find a new life with the Hudson's Bay Company, opening up the Snake River country in Oregon and company outposts in Washington. He was posted to New Caledonia—the British Columbia interior—in 1842. He was thirty-seven.

McLean took to the West. He was a big, handsome, confident red-headed man with a full beard, quick to anger, slow to forgive, and always ready to dispense his own brand of justice. "Club law," it was called in the Hudson's Bay Company—an immediate, brutal settling of accounts.

When a company aide was killed in the winter of 1849, allegedly by a young Chilcotin Indian named Tlel, McLean joined the party hunting him down. They found Tlel's uncle in a Carrier village near Quesnel, but the uncle said he didn't know where Tlel was.

So McLean shot him dead. Another man, and a baby, died at the hands of the party.

McLean showed no remorse. He wrote to his supervisor about what should be done with Tlel and any accomplices when they were caught: "Hang first, and then call a jury to find them guilty or not guilty."

But times were changing. McLean's independence and brutality were going out of fashion as ranchers and railwaymen and miners replaced the fur traders. And McLean was a difficult man, reluctant to accept authority, even insubordinate. By 1860, he was called to company regional headquarters in Victoria in an attempt to bring him under control. But he was not a man to be controlled, or to live in a place like Victoria, a hardscrabble outpost with dreams of a civilized future.

Within a year, McLean resigned. He returned to a ranch he had established northwest of Cache Creek, on Bonaparte Creek, prospecting for gold and running a roadhouse for travellers on the new Cariboo Road running to the gold boom town of Barkerville.

McLean already had married once, lived with other women, and fathered at least six children by the time he was posted to New Caledonia.

But in 1854, he had married Sophia Grant, a Native woman from the Colville reservation in Washington, south of the Okanagan. Their first son, Allan, was born a year later. Four other children—two daughters and two sons—followed. McLean was, by all accounts, a loving father to all his children.

But still a hard man. So in 1864, when Tsilhqot'in (Chilcotin) Indians killed nineteen men on crews pushing a road from Bute Inlet through their territories in a series of clashes, McLean was quick to join the colonial government force charged with putting down the uprising.

McLean was forty-nine. Old at the time. But he was ready for battle, and rode out wearing his trademark iron breastplate, designed to block bullets.

It wasn't enough. On July 17, scouting alone in defiance of the orders of the expedition's head, McLean was shot in the back and died.

McLean's family was left in a bad way. Alex was nine, Charlie was two, and Archie just a baby. The £100 pension for his widow, Sophia, would only be paid for five years.

And McLean's sister refused to recognize his marriage to an Indian, and claimed the estate.

Sophia and the children stayed on the ranch for three years, then moved to Kamloops in 1867. They were poor, and outsiders. McLean had made no friends in the Native community by killing Tlel and by his general heavy-handedness. The whites wanted nothing to do with Sophia and McLean's "half-breed" children.

So the boys grew up fast, and hard. As soon as they were able, they signed on as ranch hands, breaking horses, moving cattle—anything to get by. They lived in the saddle, slept where they could.

And, with each year, they shed a few more bonds of civilization. Work was scarce in the Kamloops region by the 1870s, when the gold boom faded. Especially for young men—or boys—like the McLeans.

So the brothers, along with Alex Hare, chose crime—stealing horses and cattle, guns and ammunition, food and anything else they wanted. If you didn't like it, they would fight you, or beat you.

There is freedom in being an outlaw, and a great sense of power. The McLeans grew bolder, their crimes more blatant.

And why not? The land was vast, and many people made their own rules.

John Ussher was the constable and jailer in Kamloops, as well as a farmer and government agent. The jail was a makeshift building that couldn't hold anyone who didn't want to be held. There was no real law.

But the Wild McLeans were going too far—stealing too boldly, challenging anyone in the way. They even threatened the life of John Andrew Mara, the powerful member of the legislative assembly for the region and owner of sprawling ranchland, claiming he had seduced their sister Annie, fathered her child, and abandoned her.

It was just a matter of time before the law could no longer turn a blind eye.

That time came in early December 1879. Rancher William Palmer was riding the hills looking for a big black horse—gelding or stallion, the accounts vary—that had been missing for several days.

Palmer found the horse. But seventeen-year-old Charlie McLean, with his teen's thin moustache, was riding it, surrounded by his armed brothers and Alex Hare.

Palmer wisely pretended not to recognize his horse, took care to give no offence, and rode to Kamloops to report the theft to Ussher.

Ussher set out to bring the McLean gang in to face the charges. He didn't expect trouble—just two men came with him on December 7, Amni Shumway, as a guide, and Palmer. John McLeod, a rancher they met on the way, agreed to join them.

Early the next day, the small posse came upon the McLeans' camp near Long Lake, about twenty-five kilometres south of Kamloops. The boys had been drinking, other people's alcohol, of course. And not a good thing.

Ussher knew the McLeans. He had dealt with them before and thought they had a relationship. He expected them to come back to Kamloops, not happily, perhaps, but peacefully. For all their threats and brawling, they had never killed anyone.

It wasn't to be. As the four men approached the camp, someone fired. It was no warning shot. The bullet hit McLeod in the cheek, wounding him. Ussher was either very brave, very foolish, or just very wrong. He walked toward the camp empty-handed, calling on the McLeans to surrender.

Alex Hare attacked him first, rushing forward with gun in one hand, knife in the other, stabbing and slashing Ussher as they struggled. Archie—just fifteen—ended the fight, shooting Ussher in the head at close range. The gunfire continued wildly from both sides for several minutes. Allan McLean was wounded, not seriously, before the three remaining members of the posse retreated, leaving Ussher's body in the snow.

The Wild McLeans had crossed a line. They took Ussher's coat and boots and guns and handcuffs and started riding south. They stole guns and food and threatened lives along the way. They killed a shepherd named James Kelly near Stump Lake, for no apparent reason.

You couldn't say they had a real plan. But Allan had married a Native woman from the Nicola Valley. He hoped that, with their haul of guns and ammunition, the McLeans could encourage the Nicola to rise up against the colonists, providing them with protection at the same time.

It didn't work. Nicola chiefs weren't interested. The McLeans were only half Native and had made few friends— Charlie had bitten off the nose of a Native man in a fight.

But back in Kamloops, the threat of an uprising, once again, seemed real. The Colony of British Columbia's 1870 census only counted non-Natives, and found a total population of 10,580. The Native population was estimated to be at least 25,000.

There were fewer than 500 people in Kamloops, still a village of squat wood-frame buildings along the Thompson River.

But a posse of about seventy men quickly formed, armed with rifles and shotguns and revolvers, and set out for the Nicola Valley to bring the McLeans to justice.

The sixty-kilometre ride was hard in the December snow, but by December 9, the posse had trapped the Wild McLeans in a rough cabin at Douglas Lake. The standoff lasted four days, with occasional shots fired on both sides.

The McLeans refused to surrender, vowed to die first. The posse camped in the snow and cold, determined to wait them out.

But their patience wore thin. The posse tried to burn the McLeans out, piling oil-soaked hay bales around the cabin, but the sodden bales wouldn't light.

What threats couldn't accomplish, hunger and thirst did. On December 13, after four days, the McLeans and Hare surrendered and were taken to Kamloops, then on to the British Columbia Penitentiary in New Westminster, a grim stone structure barely a year old.

On March 13, 1880, judge Henry Crease began their trial. Crease reminded the jury that the McLeans had a hard life, young men of mixed race with no father, cast out by both Native and white societies.

None of that mattered. A week later they were sentenced to hang. An appeal brought a second trial, and the same verdict.

The McLeans lived through one more Christmas—by all accounts troublesome and rebellious prisoners to the end, plotting escapes up to the last moment.

But in the last week of January, 1881, prison workers began building the gallows. On January 31, the three brothers and Alex Hare were hung together.

POSTSCRIPT

Allan McLean's son, George, was left to live with his mother and the Nicola Valley Natives, fatherless like Allan before him. He chose the discipline of a military life.

George was at Vimy Ridge in 1917. He captured nineteen German soldiers and killed five more who were trying to reach a machine gun, winning the Distinguished Conduct Medal.

George returned to a hero's welcome in Kamloops that October, with cheering crowds greeting his train. He stepped down from the railcar just a few hundred yards from where the posse rallied to hunt down his father.

VANISHED

It was a Sunday morning in January, still dark at 7:00 a.m.

Marguerite Telesford pulled on a pair of red sweatpants, black leg warmers, and a baggy sweatshirt. She grabbed her earmuffs—it was cold and drizzling—and went out for her regular run.

And vanished.

Telesford was athletic, tall, and slender, a twenty-year-old former track athlete and gymnast. She ran every other day, despite her busy life—studying to be a teacher, working part-time in a greeting card store, volunteering to help handicapped children.

She lived in Saanich, the largest of Greater Victoria's patchwork of municipalities. Her regular route offered a beautiful run along a quiet road through the rural Blenkinsop Valley, then back through Mount Douglas Park under towering trees.

But on January 18, 1987, she never came home.

Telesford still lived with Norma and Bill Cowell, the foster parents who took her in at fifteen. Telesford's family had migrated from Tobago; when her parents' marriage split up, she and her mother moved to Victoria. But her mother, poor and unwell, had to give up custody. The Cowells had become family.

Norma Cowell heard Telesford set out on her run, and kept listening for her return. As time passed, she grew more concerned. She called Saanich police.

She was right to be worried. Two other joggers had already spotted what looked like blood and a pair of broken earmuffs on a quiet stretch of Telesford's route. Houses there were set back from the road, which was lined with trees and brush.

Police confirmed that the stains were blood. Their search of the area found a shotgun shell and a pry bar. A hair on the earmuffs appeared to be from a black person. Marguerite was black. Neighbours reported hearing shots that morning—not uncommon as hunters targeted deer in the valley. But ominous that day.

Police and friends searched the route. A helicopter hunted from the air, while police went door-to-door, and dogs and officers with thermal-imaging scanners hunted for any sign of Telesford. At dawn Wednesday, 250 volunteers turned up to do a shoulder-to-shoulder search of rugged Mount Douglas Park—and found nothing.

As winter turned into spring, the trail appeared to have gone cold. Rewards for information climbed to more than $10,000. Police conducted more than 2,500 interviews. Desperate, they even brought in a seventy-four-year-old man who had used his "dowsing stick" to find a missing hunter in the Kootenay region. Saanich police periodically appealed for help through the spring and early summer.

But in fact, officers had targeted a prime suspect by late February. One who wasn't going anywhere. Scott MacKay, a twenty-four-year-old roofer, was locked up in the Wilkinson Road provincial jail just five kilometres from the murder scene.

MacKay had been arrested February 18, caught by police in the act of assaulting a young black woman on an Oak Bay beach. He was already facing charges for unlawfully confining a woman in January 1986 and a vicious sexual assault ten months later. But at a November 29 bail hearing on the initial sexual assault charge, Crown prosecutors failed to oppose his release.

Wilkie, as it was known in crime circles, was a foreboding brick building more than seventy years old, with a mix of offenders serving sentences of less than two years and prisoners awaiting trial. It was crowded and noisy and prisoners had little to do. So they talked and gossiped and plotted.

Soon they started to gossip about MacKay. And police got their first break in a case that was increasingly looking impossible to solve.

On February 27, a Crime Stoppers' staffer called Saanich police. A Wilkie inmate had reported MacKay was involved in Telesford's murder. The same morning, Oak Bay Police Sgt. Harold McNeill got a call from a guard who said an inmate told him MacKay was talking about the murder and saying he needed to get rid of his truck. MacKay hated blacks, the informant added.

But the police had a problem. The Oak Bay police had already searched the truck, found nothing, and released it. McNeill met with two senior officers at the Saanich Police Department. They agreed they didn't have enough information to get a legal search warrant. So they decided to gamble, seize the truck anyway, and hope any evidence would be admissible in court.

They towed the truck from MacKay's girlfriend's house to the Oak Bay police compound. It sat there for four days, until a corporal from the Saanich crime scene unit searched it. He found a blue pompom, the kind that might come from a ski hat, wedged underneath the truck's frame. There was a single hair on the pompom, which analysis found was "similar" to hair from Telesford's comb.

It wasn't much. Telesford's foster father, Bill Cowell, said the pompom looked something like one attached to a toque in a box of winter clothes kept in a hallway closet in their home. It was now missing. But he had never seen Marguerite wear it. He hadn't seen anyone wear it in the last year.

But behind the tall fences and razor wire at the Wilkie jail, developments were unfolding in the favour of the police.

MacKay wasn't popular. And Danny Cain, a thirty-one-year-old career criminal who headed the inmate committee, had a particular dislike for MacKay, who had viciously raped a friend. Cain had spent most of his life in jail and accepted the code that treated sex offenders as the lowest of the low.

He developed a plan to befriend MacKay, get him to talk about the crime, and then turn him in. Other inmates had similar ideas, some encouraged by Cain.

Their testimony would be critical at the trial to come.

Police could find no more physical evidence. By April 1988, sixteen months after the disappearance, prosecutors decided they were ready to try for a conviction.

On April 20, officers showed up at Kent Maximum Security Penitentiary, where MacKay was serving a twelve-year term for the earlier sexual assault, and told him he was charged with murdering Marguerite Telesford. During the five-hour drive and ferry ride to Victoria, officers questioned him. He denied knowing anything about Telesford's disappearance.

Crown prosecutor Dennis Murray had a tough case. There was no body. The only physical evidence was the pompom, a hair, a shotgun shell, and a pry bar. No eyewitnesses, just second-hand testimony from other criminals. No DNA results. No fingerprints. No motive.

But on January 18, 1989, two years to the day since Marguerite Telesford had vanished, the Crown set out to create a vivid picture of the crime for the Victoria jury.

The trial unfolded over two weeks. Witnesses told about the pompom with a single hair found trapped on the underside of MacKay's truck. An expert said the hair was from a black person and "similar" to a hair on Telesford's brush.

Defence lawyer Gary Kinar established that police had searched the truck previously and found nothing, and that there was no other evidence—no blood, no fibres, no damage—even though the prosecutors claimed MacKay had run Telesford down, shot her, and then driven away with her body.

The Crown's case rested on the testimony of Danny Cain and four other inmates called to testify that MacKay had, in one way or another, admitted killing Telesford. Cain, a career criminal serving a term for armed robbery, testified in handcuffs. He was considered a dangerous man. He acknowledged being a "rat" was frowned on in prison, but said it was the right thing to do in this case.

But the inmate witnesses weren't just motivated by a sense of right and wrong. The jury heard that prosecutors had agreed to drop drug trafficking and fraud charges against Cain's wife in return for his testimony.

But the prosecutors failed to disclose that the inmates had all received relocation expenses in return for their testimony, or that they had agreed to Cain's request to be transferred from Wilkie. Two other inmates testified for the defence, saying Cain had set out to frame MacKay.

And MacKay took the stand, serious in dark-rimmed glasses, grey pants, and a brown tweed jacket. I didn't do it, MacKay insisted, saying he was being framed.

Prosecutor Dennis Murray painted a vivid picture in his closing address. "What happened here was an execution," he told the jury. MacKay accosted Telesford. He knocked her down with his truck, then drove over her. She tried to crawl away, and MacKay got out of his truck and hit her with the iron bar found at the scene and shot her twice.

It was vivid, and damning, even if there was no evidence to support the theory. And after fifteen hours of deliberation, the jury found MacKay guilty of first-degree murder. He was sentenced to life in prison, with no chance of parole for twenty-five years.

POSTSCRIPT

On appeal, the conviction on first-degree murder was overturned, with the court ruling there was no evidence that showed planning or premeditation as the Crown had claimed. MacKay's life sentence was unchanged, but the court ruled he could be eligible for parole in fifteen years.

MacKay's parole applications have been denied. He remains in jail, and maintains his innocence.

Marguerite Telesford's body has never been found.

MURDER AT SEA

Drugs and sex. Death in a cruise ship penthouse. Mysterious changes to a will. Odd characters. And money—lots and lots of money.

When Robert Frisbee was charged with murder, it was like something out of the movies. In fact, when Frisbee's defence lawyer (and novelist) William Deverell was asked if he planned to use the case as the basis for a book, he said no. "Fiction has to be believable."

And Frisbee's life story was hard to believe.

He was born in Springfield, Massachusetts, on May 5, 1927, but not as Robert Frisbee. That would come much later. He was Robert Dion. His difficult father eventually left the family.

Young Robert didn't fit in. He knitted, fanatically. He was bad at sports, effeminate, small—and, unsurprisingly—teased. He wanted to learn shorthand and enrolled in a high school that was almost entirely female. He joined the girls' choir. He would tell a doctor years later that he had been sexually abused by his older brother.

By his early teens, Robert had embarked on gay relationships with older men. By sixteen, he had hooked up with a New York grifter named Tom Leary, who proposed using Robert as the bait in a scheme to shake down closeted gays.

Luckily, the army came calling. Robert was drafted at age eighteen in August 1945, weeks before the Second World War ended. A short marriage produced a son who died in infancy and Robert's belated realization—or acceptance—that he was gay.

He was a poor soldier. A girlish underhand attempt at tossing a hand grenade, like a bad softball pitch, produced much screaming from his sergeant. But he was an adequate army clerk until his discharge.

Leary was waiting, with a new scam selling fake work papers to jobless naval veterans. He flew Robert to San Francisco to start the business there. But Leary was arrested, and Robert had to make his own way in the city by the bay.

It didn't take long.

Robert was charming and acquiescent, if a little awkward in social situations. At a party, he met Dwight Frisbee, the rich son of a New England lumber baron with no apparent occupation.

Frisbee's chauffeur had quit, taking the car with him, and Robert was hired on the spot as a replacement. Charming acquiescence paid off. And perhaps his age helped. Frisbee was forty-eight, Robert just twenty-one.

Robert was happy. He didn't have to look for work, or reveal just how little he knew of the world.

He had wondered what it would be like to be rich, with no particular ambition. Now he found out, and he enjoyed it very much indeed. Robert and Dwight shared a house in a posh San Francisco neighbourhood. Dwight's family income allowed servants and days of cocktails and fine food, parties with friends. And more cocktails. Robert discovered how much he enjoyed cocktails.

But his personality never changed as he drank. He was always quiet, agreeable Robert, shying away from unpleasantness or confrontation. Wanting everyone to be happy.

The two became lovers, for a time. (Frisbee, like Robert, had been married, but found it did not suit him.)

But Frisbee, nearing fifty, had always wanted a son. After two years together, he adopted his twenty-three-year-old partner and chauffeur. Robert Dion became Robert Frisbee. The adoption also ensured Robert would be looked after when Dwight died.

Dwight took the new relationship seriously. It would be wrong to keep having sex with a son, he told Robert. That was over.

But Robert had a new, odd love interest. Daniel Kazakes was a failed developer, with a mail-order certificate saying he was a reverend and claimed psychic powers, who sometimes ran struggling little import shops. Kazakes and Robert became lovers, with the approval of Dwight Frisbee and Kazakes's wife, Irene.

Robert continued to care for his increasingly unwell adoptive father. When Dwight died at fifty-eight, in part because of his drinking, he left Robert a house and $160,000—real money then, when the average income was $3,700. Enough to last a lifetime.

But Robert wasn't good with money. The inheritance was mostly gone—"squandered," a court decision sniffed—within a few years. Robert's prospects diminished. He found himself a man of limited means and no real occupation, living with the Kazakeses. It was discouraging.

But around 1964, Dwight Frisbee's ex-wife came to the rescue. She introduced Robert to her older friends Phillip and Muriel Barnett. Phillip was a successful attorney with investments and business interests, Muriel at the centre of society life. Together, the couple floated through San Francisco society, eating at the right restaurants and showing up at the charity balls and symphonies.

Robert just drifted into the Barnetts' employ. He was a charming, unobtrusive guest when Muriel needed an extra man to fill out the table at a dinner party, always ready to run errands or drive them somewhere. He became sort of a secretary-assistant at first, but was soon doing everything—driving them, planning parties, pouring drinks, joining them for breakfasts and dinner parties.

Having sex with Phillip.

Part staff. Part friend. Part pet.

Robert was charming. Odd, with his habit of referring to himself in the third person, and his determined desire to please. Passive, agreeable, never arguing. A gentle soul, every-one agreed. Perhaps too accommodating and easily taken advantage of, some thought quietly.

And he was good looking, with swept-back hair and smiling eyes, although a bit the worse for the drink. With an expression, often, that made it appear he feared he would be hit if he wasn't useful or amusing, or both.

When Phillip Barnett died at eighty-five in 1984, Robert believed he would be looked after in the will, and that Barnett had promised a bequest that would give him independence.

Instead, he was sentenced to more servitude. Phillip left his millions to his wife, stipulating only that when she died, Frisbee should get $250,000. Most of the estate, Phillip directed, should then go to fund a chair at the University of San Francisco Law School. Muriel had her lawyer draft her own will, incorporating Phillip's requests.

Robert was fifty-seven. He had become used to a luxuri-ous lifestyle, had no money or skills, and was an alcoholic. So he continued as Muriel's factotum, dinner date, and drinking companion, living in a nearby apartment with Kazakes. He had power over bank accounts and paid her bills. They started each day with a cocktail, and generally never stopped drinking.

It was no surprise that in October, seven months after Phillip's death, Muriel had a drunken fall in her bedroom and injured her neck. In hospital, Robert said later, she decided to change her will and had him draft an amendment. Two-thirds of her estate—probably $2 million—would go to him. Her sig-nature on the handwritten codicil was witnessed by Kazakes and one of their friends.

Their lives of socializing, spending, alcohol, and misadven-ture rolled on. A grand tour of Europe ended abruptly when Robert's ill-considered attempt to quit drinking cold turkey left him unconscious in a posh London hotel. They returned to San Francisco.

But once Robert recovered—he tried not drinking for a while, but it didn't stick—Muriel booked an Alaska cruise for August 1985.

But before leaving, she instructed her lawyer to draw up a revised will that she could sign on her return from the cruise. It added a few small bequests—and restored the $250,000 bequest to Robert, not the $2 million he had been counting on.

Robert and Muriel shared a $2,000-a-day penthouse on the *Royal Viking Star*, a cruise ship targeting the luxury market. (Separate beds, of course.) A butler was at their service, and Muriel was chuffed to learn Elizabeth Taylor had recently slept in the same bed.

On August 19, the ship docked in Victoria. Muriel, Robert, and two friends hired a limousine and driver to see Craigdarroch Castle and Butchart Gardens. Robert helped Muriel back on board around 4:30 p.m., and they arranged to meet the other couple for pre-dinner drinks before the captain's farewell dinner.

In the cabin, Robert mixed drinks to prepare them for the evening. French 75s, a potent combination of gin and champagne. (The cocktail, invented in Paris in 1915, got its name because it packed the kick of the French army's 75-mm field gun.) He took a couple of Librium, a sedative, had a bath, drank another French 75, and fell asleep, he said.

At 6:45 p.m., Michael Michael, the improbably named butler, arrived as usual with caviar. Frisbee heard the knock, he said, went to wake Muriel, and found her in a kneeling position beside her blood-soaked bed, her head battered at least four times. "She is dead," he told Michael.

Frisbee was distraught, and somewhat drunk. "I don't know what happened, I was asleep," he told the ship's doctor.

The ship sailed on to San Francisco. Police were waiting for Robert.

He was a good suspect. He had a motive, if he believed Barnett planned to sign a new will that would cut his $2-million inheritance to $250,000.

And it seemed impossible that a stranger had decided to kill Barnett on a cruise ship. Especially with Robert sleeping in a bed less than one metre away.

Murder on the high seas is complicated. The FBI and U.S. authorities spent months working on the case before they decided the *Royal Viking Star* had still been in Canadian waters when Barnett was bludgeoned.

Finally, on December 2, 1986, Frisbee's murder trial began in front of a jury in British Columbia Supreme Court.

Deverell and the defence team faced an enormous challenge. A Victoria jury would be confounded by the whole story, entirely foreign to their experience. Frisbee had a motive, a history of small thefts from Muriel, and was the only logical killer. He was there.

And Frisbee could not deny killing her, because he said he remembered nothing of the critical hours.

The defence argued the prosecutors hadn't proved Frisbee was the killer. But if the jury decided he had killed her, then the defence maintained he was in a state of "non-insane automatism." He did not know what he was doing.

There was a rather large problem—Robert Frisbee. He had, foolishly, written what he called notes for a novel based on his case while locked up in San Francisco. They were seized by the police and, at least, raised doubts about his innocence.

It took the jury ten hours to find Robert Frisbee guilty of first-degree murder on January 10, 1987. An appeal reduced that to second-degree murder, and he was sentenced to life imprisonment without the chance of parole for ten years.

But Frisbee never made a parole hearing. Less than four years later, on July 25, 1991, Frisbee died of liver cancer in the Matsqui Institution prison hospital. He was sixty-four.

THE BOOGEYMAN

It was hard not to expect the worst when the Amber Alert went out at suppertime on a warm September evening in 2011.

Three-year-old Kienan Hebert had vanished from his home in Sparwood, a quiet coal-mining town in eastern British Columbia, almost at the Alberta border.

His parents had tucked the cute redhead into bed Tuesday night wearing his blue Scooby Doo boxer shorts. He shared his room with his six-year-old brother.

In the morning, Kienan was gone.

When police identified a suspect, things looked even worse.

Randall Hopley was a scrawny, forty-six-year-old loner, with a long criminal record—including sexual assault—who lived in a ratty trailer. For decades, a succession of doctors and counsellors had warned that Hopley was a threat and needed treatment. Nothing was ever done.

Police released photos showing an unshaven boy-man, with puffy face, high forehead, bad bowl haircut, and blotchy skin. The expression in his green eyes was at once puzzled and a bit angry.

As newspapers dug into Hopley's background, the picture grew grimmer.

His criminal record went back decades. Just three years earlier, Hopley had been sent to jail for eighteen months for a break-in that was part of a plan to kidnap a ten-year-old mentally challenged boy. In 1985, he had been convicted of sexual assault on a five-year-old boy.

Now he had snatched a toddler from his bed and vanished.

Kienan's parents, Paul and Tammy Hebert, were regulars at Sparwood Fellowship Baptist Church.

They went to great lengths to protect their eight children. Tammy was a stay-at-home mom, while Paul worked in real estate. They rarely went out and never hired babysitters. The children were even home-schooled, to keep them from risks. "Protection is what we wanted," Paul Hebert said. "We didn't want to put them in the public school system for safety."

Not everyone feared the worst. Margaret Fink, Hopley's seventy-year-old mother, said her son wouldn't hurt Kienan.

"I feel really sorry for the little kid," she said. "I don't think Randy will harm him. He's been with the grandkids here a lot and he's been pretty good."

Hopley visited her in Fernie hours before Kienan went missing, she said, the first time after his latest stint in jail. They had tea. "He gave me a big hug. He said he was doing all right."

The RCMP launched a massive manhunt, with more than sixty officers working the case. Tips flooded in. Roadblocks checked every vehicle at key points in the area.

But Hopley and Kienan had vanished.

On Saturday—four days after they had last seen him—Kienan's parents met with the media, sitting at a folding table under a white tent outside the Sparwood fire hall. They faced the cameras and microphones, but they were really trying to speak directly to Hopley.

Paul Hebert, a big man with close-cropped grey hair, spoke, while Tammy sat beside him. Both battled tears.

"We're just asking, please bring Kienan to a safe place right now, okay? Like a gas station or a store parking lot where he can be visibly seen and you can just drop him off there. Walk away. We just want him safe."

"Kienan is only three years old right now.... He can't tell us who you are," said Hebert, unshaven and wearing the same purple shirt he had for days. "This is your chance, right now, to get away. All we want is for Kienan to come back with us and to be safe in our arms again."

It was desperate, heartbreaking. And it worked.

The Heberts had moved temporarily to a neighbour's house. A search headquarters was located on the only road into the subdivision. RCMP officers were everywhere.

But somehow, around 2:00 a.m. Sunday, Hopley took Kienan back to his home, settled him in a big, comfy brown armchair, and tucked blankets around him. Then he left and called 911 to make sure the RCMP would know Kienan was there.

Paul and Tammy found their son asleep, unharmed. An ending no one expected.

A few hours later, Kienan was having fun on the front lawn of the tidy two-storey home with his brothers and sisters, playing with a Frisbee, a balloon, and an aerosol can that shot bright lines of foamy string. He had been away playing with "Jason," he told police.

The officers in charge decided to reach out to Hopley again, calling a press conference to thank him, and urge him to surrender.

But the hunt continued. Hopley wouldn't go far, acquaintances said. He loved the woods and mountains, was at home there. And anyway, he mostly lived on welfare and had no money to get away.

Someone like Hopley could disappear into the mountains. If he could keep quiet.

Hopley couldn't. He heard the news reports and knew they were all wrong. He was no monster.

Hopley began posting on Facebook pages devoted to Kienan's disappearance. He apologized to the family, promised he hadn't hurt Kienan, and said they had water, heat, food, and TV in their hideout. Kienan was happy and cheerful, he wrote, and in fact kept Hopley's spirits up.

Hopley wanted the world to know it wasn't just some senseless act. It was a desperate bid to win attention for his wrongful conviction in the 2008 case involving the attempted abduction of the ten-year-old boy. He was forced into that crime. The boy's birth mother offered him money and threatened to make up sex crime allegations if he refused.

He promised to turn himself in once he had seen a lawyer.

The Facebook posts were the break the police needed. They traced the Internet account to a summer Bible camp in Coleman, just across the Alberta border. Officers set up surveillance and, on September 13, a week after Kienan was taken, they spotted Hopley running from a cabin at a nearby mine site. A police dog was unleashed, and he was captured (and bitten).

Inside the cabin, police found food, a TV and kids' DVDs, children's clothes, a camp stove—and a *Today's Parent* magazine.

Paul Hebert had questions. Why was Hopley on the street when the courts had judged him a danger in 1985? They should either have got him help or locked him up, he said, but did neither. "If a doctor can get malpractice, why can't a judge?"

But the problem wasn't a judge. The justice system—the child protection system—failed Hopley, and society.

Pore through the files and the story emerges. Hopley had a troubled childhood. He was, in the language of the day, slow. (Later assessments assessed his IQ from sixty-eight to at best "borderline normal.")

His father died in a mine explosion when he was two; his mother said he always seemed to be angry after that. His childhood was split between foster homes and his mother's house, grim for a child already insecure and unable to handle change.

The first indication that Hopley really needed help came when he was eight, and an assessment recommended he receive special institutional care.

That never happened.

Hopley made it through grade ten in a special education program, but with no skills—no social skills, life skills, or any sort of trade.

In his final foster home, when he was fifteen and sixteen, he sexually assaulted three younger children—a girl and two boys. He was charged and sent for assessments, which were uniformly bleak.

One doctor listed Hopley's problems—emotional deprivation, behavioural disturbances, poor social skills, lack of empathy, and an inability even to understand why people were upset when he molested younger children.

But, the doctor said, there was nowhere to send Hopley for help.

A second assessment produced similar results and found he needed treatment. But there was no room in the recommended program.

His foster parents persisted, and Hopley was referred to a psychologist at the University of British Columbia, who saw him for eight treatment sessions. She was gloomy about his future too.

"It is unlikely that Randy will refrain from assaulting children without treatment," she reported. "The boy is not clever, not attractive, and not socially skilled; he is unlikely to attract girls of his own age. Children, who are basically powerless to reject him, are an obvious alternative."

The psychologist said that treatment might not work. But without it, Hopley was highly likely to victimize more children.

Hopley didn't get treatment.

And, like all children in British Columbia government care then and now, he was pushed out of the foster home on his nineteenth birthday, without support. It's a difficult transition for any youth. It was predictably disastrous for Hopley.

He was almost immediately arrested for possession of stolen property, and placed on probation.

A few months later, in May 1985, Hopley was riding his bicycle on a Fernie path when he saw a five-year-old boy, pushed him down, and sexually assaulted him. When the boy began to cry, Hopley stopped and let him go. He was quickly arrested.

A doctor assessed him and recommended treatment in a sex offender program. That did not happen.

Instead, Hopley was sentenced to two years, received no specialized treatment, and refused to participate in available programs.

When his release date neared, a psychiatrist recommended consistent supervision in a community-based support facility.

That did not happen.

The parole board directed Corrections Canada to find "an adult residential facility with firm external control over the behaviour of residents together with intensive supervision on site."

That did not happen.

Amazingly, Hopley wasn't convicted of any more sexual offences.

But he bounced in and out of jail, for crimes that reflected a lack of intelligence, impulse control, and morality. He broke into houses and businesses, stole things, lived in other people's cabins. When he caught a break and received probation, he ignored the conditions and landed in court again.

"Ultimately it gets down to straight locking you up for no better purpose than to keep you out of other people's homes and their business," a provincial court judge told Hopley before sending him, once again, to jail.

This time, Supreme Court Justice Heather Holmes had to figure out what to do with Hopley.

The Hebert family had left the province and didn't participate. Paul had met Hopley, and Tammy had sent him notes. They were Christians, Paul explained. They practised forgiveness.

But Holmes said Hopley had done great damage to the family.

Hopley had "made the boogeyman real" in their lives.

On November 29, 2013, Holmes sentenced Hopley to six years and two months for taking Kienan and breaking into the Hebert home. With time he had spent in custody, he would serve just under four years. Enough time, Holmes said, for him to get help in prison. She declared Hopley a long-term offender and ordered supervision for ten years after he is released.

Maybe this time Hopley will get treatment. Maybe the system will work.

Nothing did for the first forty-six years of his life.

DEADLY MASSACRE

I t was the only war fought in British Columbia. It lasted less than fifteen weeks in the spring and summer of 1864 and claimed twenty-six lives. One side—the British colonies— never even acknowledged it was a war.

But for Klatasassin, the charismatic Tsilhqot'in leader, fighting white road builders pushing into traditional territory was war, and a desperate effort to save his people.

It was probably inevitable that Natives and arriving Europeans would clash violently. The breaking point came in the dense forests above Bute Inlet, some 240 kilometres up the coast from Vancouver. Hunger, greed, desperation, gold fever, and smallpox came together to set the stage for conflict.

By 1860, the first gold rush to the Lower Fraser River had exhausted all the easy claims. But prospectors were striking it rich in the Cariboo, attracting a new wave of would-be gold miners.

The new fields were harder to reach, requiring 500 kilometres of gruelling overland travel. Packing supplies in was expensive, and basic goods cost a fortune in the remote goldfields. A shovel could cost fourteen dollars, almost a typical week's wage.

Alfred Waddington, a sixty-year-old entrepreneur and politician who arrived in Victoria for the first gold rush in 1858, saw opportunity. He proposed to cut the land journey almost in half by carving a road through the coastal mountains from Bute Inlet to the Cariboo. Supplies would be carried by sea to the inlet.

Waddington, a peculiar-looking man with a long face, high forehead, and close-set eyes, lined up investors, promising big profits from tolls on the road, and won government support.

It was a crazy idea. The first survey party, in 1861, found the route through the narrow Homathco Canyon incredibly difficult, and the seven members almost died after their canoe was destroyed in rapids. They were saved, half-starved, by friendly Tsilhqot'in, and made their way out in a roughly carved dugout.

But the physical barriers were not the only problem.

The Tsilhqot'in—like their coastal neighbours—were facing hard times in the early 1860s, with food in short supply. They had much less contact with Europeans than many First Nations. Hudson's Bay Company efforts to build trade with the Tsilhqot'in since the 1820s had failed.

The Tsilhqot'in had good reason to fear any incursion into their territory. Settlers or miners could take their land or kill or drive away scarce game.

And they could bring horrible death.

On March 12, 1862, the steamship *Brother Jonathan* arrived from San Francisco, two paddlewheels churning the waters of Victoria's harbour as it pulled into the dock opposite the Songhees Indian settlement. The sixty-seven-metre-long ship, under sail and steam, had made the trip from San Francisco in three days, bringing 350 passengers, mostly in search of gold.

One passenger was sick, infected with smallpox. The disease was devastating. An 1830s epidemic had killed thousands and wiped out entire First Nations communities.

Now it was back. Spreading through Victoria, carried onto the mainland and into the interior by gold seekers. By July, it had reached the Tsilhqot'in.

* * *

Waddington's surveyors and road builders found progress painfully slow. In March 1864, as ice came off the rivers, they arrived to try and push the project forward, building on the thirty-seven kilometres of road and trail completed in the previous year.

Waddington was desperate. The company had collapsed and investors had fled. He had sold everything he owned in a last bid to finish the road to the goldfields.

William Brewster was foreman of the fifteen-man crew. He felt the pressure.

But things immediately began to go wrong. He was counting on supplies left over from the previous year to help provision the crew. But it had been a hard, hungry winter for Natives living around the work camp. They had broken into a storehouse and stolen twenty-five big sacks of flour.

Brewster was angry and determined to find out who was responsible. But none of the Natives would talk.

But he had leverage. The road crew hired Tsilhqot'in packers. When a group of families came looking for work, he gave them an ultimatum: No work unless they told him who stole the flour. That failed. So Brewster told them they could work—but their wages would be docked to pay for the flour, even if they hadn't taken it.

Now everyone was angry. You're in our territory, a Tsilhqot'in man said. You owe us. (The road had reached inland to traditional Tsilhqot'in lands.)

Challenges and accusations went back and forth. Then Brewster went too far. Unless you do what I want, he said, the Tsilhqot'in will die. The whites will unleash disease. For people who had seen the devastation of smallpox and knew it was once more on the land, it was a deadly threat.

The standoff stalled. The Tsilhqot'in stayed around. And, within a few days, Brewster hired them to work on the road.

But word of the confrontation reached Piell, the fifteen-year-old son of Klatsassin. He told his father of the threat.

Klatsassin was a leader of Tsilhqot'in warriors in fights with other First Nations. Strong, about forty, with piercing eyes and a square jaw. He decided war was the only response to the threat to spread smallpox.

On April 28, the first casualty was claimed. Klatsassin and a small group of family and supporters reached a ferry across the Homathco River set up by the road builders. He demanded food and blankets; ferryman Tim Smith refused. That evening,

Klatsassin killed Smith with his musket, and his body was thrown in the river.

The opening shot had been fired. Klatsassin and a larger group of warriors spent the next day preparing for battle. Early on the morning of April 30, they attacked the road building crew's main camp.

Twelve men were sleeping in six tents when Klatsassin's group attacked with muskets, axes, and clubs. In minutes, the ground was soaked with blood and nine men were dead. The three survivors, wounded, took three days to reach Bute Inlet.

The Tsilhqot'in party knew Brewster and three other members of the road crew were blazing a trail about six kilometres away. They killed them all. Brewster was shot, hit with an axe in the head, and mutilated.

For Klatsassin, it was a day of victories on the field of battle. But when the news reached Victoria almost two weeks later, the *Daily Colonist* headlined the story with two words—"Deadly Massacre." Over the next month, a homesteader and three men running a pack train were killed by the Tsilhqot'in.

In Victoria and New Westminster, officials of the colonies of Vancouver Island and British Columbia saw the uprising as a real threat.

Two Royal Navy ships and almost 150 men were sent to put down the rebellion.

The forests and mountains defeated the colonial force, largely composed of paid civilians. Progress was painfully slow, and provisions quickly exhausted. The Tsilhqot'in seemed to vanish.

But Klatsassin and his party, which included women and children, were suffering as well. Summer would soon end, food was scarce, and the group was ill-prepared for winter.

On August 15, eight Tsilhqot'in warriors, including Klatsassin, walked into the Chilko River camp of one of the colonial expeditions. They believed they had been promised a chance to meet British Columbia governor Frederick Seymour and discuss terms of surrender. Seymour had arrived to take up his post just two weeks before the killings, and insisted on joining the expedition.

Instead, they were arrested.

The Tsilhqot'in were taken to Quesnelmouth, as Quesnel was then known, and brought before Matthew Begbie — later known as the "Hanging Judge." In fact, Begbie spoke several Native languages and had, four years earlier, found a California man guilty of assaulting an Aboriginal man solely on the basis of testimony from other Natives, an unprecedented ruling.

Begbie was troubled by the way the men were persuaded to surrender. In the south, critics—including Waddington's business and political rivals—said Brewster and the road crew created the problems by mistreating the Tsilhqot'in.

Ultimately, none of that mattered. Five of the eight, including Klatsassin, were found guilty of murder. They were hung together on October 26 at dawn on a cold morning. About 250 people showed up to watch the wooden trap doors open as one, and the ropes snapped tight.

POSTSCRIPT

The Tsilhqot'in never gave up on defending their territory, though the battlegrounds evolved, moving from the forests of British Columbia's northwest into the wood-paneled court-rooms of the cities.

In 2014, the Tsilhqot'in emerged victorious from a 21-year legal battle, as the Supreme Court of Canada granted them title to their traditional territories. The court found the Tsilhqot'in—like many British Columbia First Nations—had never signed treaties or ceded the right to their land. The precedent-setting ruling granted the Tsilhqot'in title to 1,700 square kilometres, the same land Klatsassin set out to defend.

THE ROCKEFELLER CON

British Columbia has seen some extraordinary con men. But no one quite like Christopher Rocancourt.

Rocancourt duped victims with the most implausible claims of riches and celebrity, donning identities like most people change their clothes. For the young Frenchman, it was a game. If the people he swindled couldn't see that he was lying, they deserved to lose their money and be humiliated. If he was caught, it was just a challenge to escape and start again.

Rocancourt was already a wanted man when he breezed into Vancouver in early 2000. He was thirty-three, and a veteran of scams and cons on two continents. He had survived a rough-and-tumble childhood in northern France, his father an alcoholic house painter and his mother a young prostitute. He spent time in an orphanage.

Still in his teens, Rocancourt set out to recreate himself. He moved to the bright lights of Paris, found friends with money, and told the world he was, implausibly, Prince de Galitzine, a rich Russian aristocrat. (He spoke no Russian.) He settled into a life of crime—cons, forgery, thefts, and even, according to police, a role in a violent $400,000 robbery of a Geneva jewelry store in 1991.

When things got too hot in Europe, Rocancourt, just twenty-three, took his act to the United States.

He landed in Los Angeles, and used charm, his French accent, and a series of fake identities to line up new victims. He was a cat burglar, he told some people. A rich international businessman. A nephew of movie producer Dino De Laurentiis. The son of Sophia Loren. Whatever worked.

And he lived the part, sharing a house with actor Mickey Rourke for a while, living in a $75,000-a-month Beverly Wilshire Hotel room, negotiating to buy a mansion, a jet, and luxury cars.

None of the deals ever closed. But they all impressed people who advanced money to invest in business deals that never seemed to happen.

So did the beautiful women who always seemed to be at Rocancourt's side. Not just his wife, Pia Reyes, a former Playmate of the Month. Girlfriends too.

He wasn't particularly good-looking. He was short—"five feet nine and a half," he always insisted—with a high forehead and prominent nose. Expensive haircuts added a certain style. "He's not an attractive man," a woman friend observed. "So I always wondered how he had his way with the ladies."

But in 1998, things were growing complicated in Los Angeles. Rocancourt went to a police station to report he had been shot at, and police discovered he was using a forged passport. He was charged, released on bail—and promptly skipped for the East Coast.

He ended up in the Hamptons, summer resort for the rich of New York, both new money and old, and wonderful hunting ground for a charming French con artist.

And between Los Angeles and the Hamptons, Rocancourt became Christopher Rockefeller, part of the famously wealthy family. He lived the part, travelling with an aide, chartering helicopters to make grand entrances, spending evenings in expensive restaurants and days shopping for a mansion.

It was easy to persuade people to loan him a little money or invest in a scheme, to dodge bills for the champagne-fuelled nights and expensive hotels and inns. He was a Rockefeller. The money was no problem.

Not everyone was fooled, though. Why would a Rockefeller have a heavy French accent? And those aides and hangers-on seemed thuggish for a wealthy young man of the world. More like crooks. Creditors inevitably grew impatient with the stories, and victims got tired of waiting for returns on their investments.

Rocancourt was arrested, facing a raft of larceny and fraud charges. He posted bail, and promptly fled with his wife and Zeus, their son.

Wanted on both coasts, Rocancourt decided a trip to Canada might be wise in 2000. And Whistler, the booming ski town with visitors from around the world, seemed just the place to find new prey.

He adopted a new identity—Michael Van Hoven—with a wonderfully brazen backstory. He was, he told new acquaintances, the son of a reclusive Dutch billionaire businessman, and was himself worth some $250 million.

But his love was car racing, and Ferrari had just signed him to a $28-million-a-year Formula One contract.

It was breathtakingly bold. Formula One is the pinnacle of motor racing. Ferrari's two F1 drivers are international celebrities. The story would have crumbled with the tiniest bit of checking.

Rocancourt turned creating his new character into an artistic exercise.

"For the look: small glasses and slicked back hair," he wrote in a memoir. "Classic, serious, sporty. Obvious character traits: high self-esteem, modesty and kindness. Of course. I tried testing out my new identity on women to observe the reaction. I remember a gorgeous saleswoman in the cashmere shop of the shopping arcade of the hotel. What a beauty! She was very impressed with Van Hoven."

The new look alone was not enough. He took a $1,500-a-night suite in the Westin Resort and Spa, and made sure he was noticed. Sometimes that meant tipping lavishly, a $100 bill for a small service. Other times, Rocancourt pushed in front of other clients and demanded special treatment, acting out the entitlement of the rich.

The trap was being set. "I established my hang-out at the Bearfoot Bistro, a fine dining restaurant with one of the best wine cellars on the continent," he wrote. He bought expensive wines, talked about his wealth, how much he loved Whistler, and his desire to buy property. It always worked.

"Usually, a real-estate agent will show up within 48 hours. And the other offers follow: 'You should invest in my business, Mr. Van Hoven—I can make you lots of money, Mr. Van Hoven.' All you have to do is choose."

It worked. A real estate agent showed Rocancourt the Chateau du Lac, a partially completed home that would be the most expensive in Whistler. I'll take it, said Rocancourt, writing a cheque for a $100,000 deposit that somehow never cleared.

That was enough to let him show off "his" new house to acquaintances, even directing the builders to make changes. Who could doubt the wealth of a man who had just bought the most expensive home in the famously high-priced Whistler real estate market?

Not Robert Baldock. The Vancouver businessman was trying to launch a company that would market a promising but unproven tool to assess mental illness by monitoring heart rates. It was a high-risk investment, and a tough sell. He was no neophyte. Baldock was about sixty, with a serious business background.

Baldock and his wife, Norma, were introduced to Rocancourt in Vancouver. He quickly came to be the white knight who would solve all the problems in launching the company.

Rocancourt assured the Baldocks that his father would invest $5 million. And they began helping him while the deal came together, advancing him money, renting him cars, buying him a $5,000 laptop, letting him use Robert's credit card. Baldock paid a mysterious lawyer to work on the deal; the "lawyer" was really Rocancourt.

Baldock even bought a $26,000 Rolex and gave it to Rocancourt, who said his father collected watches and would be delighted by the gift.

The $5 million never came. The excuses should have set off alarm bells. Rocancourt told Baldock he missed one meeting because he had to fly to Brazil to race for Ferrari.

But Baldock wanted to believe. So much that he twice flew to Geneva for meetings with Rocancourt's non-existent father, and accepted his excuses when the meetings never took place.

Rocancourt liked to cast himself as a kind of Robin Hood, stealing from the rich and greedy.

In fact, he preyed on anyone who crossed his path.

Katie Olver was a twenty-four-year-old front-desk clerk at the Westin when she crossed paths with Rocancourt, who befriended Katie and her boyfriend, Jon Reader. She was Australian; her boyfriend was British. Rocancourt was a generous friend, picking up the tab for fancy dinners and nights on the town and letting them stay in his suite when he was away. He and his beautiful wife seemed like real friends.

So when Rocancourt said he had connections and could help them get green cards so they could travel and work in the United States, they were glad to hand over their passports and $475 each for the fees.

And they didn't think it odd when Rocancourt, saying he had to rush to the United Kingdom on business and didn't have time to exchange money, asked if they could give him a few thousand pounds. They gave him almost all their money—about £3,000, some $6,500. Rocancourt said he'd have $10,000 deposited into their account, a nice return.

Olver and Reader needed the money. They were about to head to the United States (though without green cards). As they drove toward Los Angeles, they kept checking their bank balance. And slowly, painfully, the couple realized they'd been had.

But they didn't yet know how badly. Until Reader tried to use his credit card and found Rocancourt had somehow obtained the number and run up $22,000 in charges. Those lavish dinners and expensive wines—they were charged to Reader's own credit card.

The Baldocks—out more than $150,000—were also growing suspicious. When they learned Rocancourt's deal to buy the Whistler mansion had fallen through, they called the RCMP.

Rocancourt could have taken off. The scam couldn't run forever. But he was greedy, calling the Baldocks, supposedly from Geneva, telling them the $5 million was almost ready.

RCMP traced the cellphone call to the Oak Bay Beach Hotel across the water in Victoria, fading but grand, and in a ritzy neighbourhood with some spectacular oceanfront mansions.

But Rocancourt wouldn't get the chance to find new victims. On April 26, 2001, Rocancourt left the hotel at 11:30 p.m. The police emergency response team was waiting.

Even in jail, Rocancourt was unrepentant, welcoming media attention, working on a book, and insulting his victims. Celebrity, it seemed, was a new kind of scam. He spent a year in a Victoria jail and used it to begin constructing a new legend—this time using his real name. He pleaded guilty to the charges in Canada and was deported to the United States, where he was sentenced to almost four years in jail.

Rocancourt used his jail time well. He revelled in a wave of publicity—TV profiles, magazine and newspaper articles. He called media—collect—from his prison cell to encourage them to write about him. And they did. He told new stories—no more likely to be true than the old ones. He became the daring, dashing gentleman thief.

It was, perhaps, Rocancourt's greatest reinvention. He claimed to have conned people out of $40 million. Even if exaggerated, that represents terrible damage to hundreds of innocent people.

But Rocancourt emerged from prison as a self-created, charming rogue and international celebrity.

Within months of his release, he showed up on the red carpet at the 2008 Cannes Film Festival, supermodel Naomi Campbell on his arm.

Rocancourt didn't have to pretend to be someone else any more.

THE BEAST

A catalogue of criminal types passes through the courts. The drunks. The addicts. People with mental illness. The bewildered first-time offenders. The career criminals.

And the evil. The extremely rare people who stare at the courtroom with cunning and menace.

Clifford Olson might be the most evil of all.

Olson was a New Year's baby in 1940, born in Vancouver and raised in Richmond, then a distant suburb. His father was a milkman, and Olson was one of four children.

He was an unlikeable child. He stole, bullied, tormented the neighbourhood pets. When he kept getting into fights at school and losing, Olson took up boxing, and used his new skills to batter the boys who had beaten him.

He made it through grade eight and became a habitual, hapless criminal, spending most of his adult life behind bars on scores of charges. He was short, stocky, and dark-haired, with squinty eyes under dark brows. He seemed a typical small-time, sleazy career criminal.

But Olson was cunning. He escaped custody seven times. He knew people's weaknesses, and the flaws in his captors' systems. He was a jailhouse lawyer, a snitch and, when he had the chance, a prison bully and sexual predator.

And he was a monster.

Christine Weller was twelve in 1980, with dark hair and a direct gaze. She was a tomboy with lots of friends. She liked hanging out in the local mall, roaming around the soon-to-be developed fields in Surrey.

But Clifford Olson knew she would be a good victim. He could always judge good victims.

When Christine didn't come back to the motel room where her family lived that rainy Monday afternoon, November 17, 1980, her parents assumed she was staying at a friend's house. They didn't report her missing for a week. There was no big police effort to find her.

On Christmas Day, a man walking his dog discovered her body near the Fraser River in Richmond. She had been stabbed repeatedly, and strangled with a belt.

It was the start of a time of terror. On April 16, Olson abducted and murdered thirteen-year-old Colleen Daignault of Surrey. Her body was found five months later. Less than a week later, Olson lured Daryn Johnsrude, sixteen, from a mall. His lifeless, beaten body was found less than two weeks later.

Olson paused to marry Joan Hale in a formal ceremony in the People's Full Gospel Chapel in Surrey, with their one-month-old son, Stephen, as a witness.

But just four days after the wedding, he spotted sixteen-year-old Sandra Wolfsteiner trying to hitchhike home. He picked her up and killed in her a patch of woods.

The children kept disappearing, and dying. Ada Court, thirteen, disappeared June 21. Simon Partington, nine, disappeared July 2 while riding his bicycle to a friend's house. Judy Kozma, fourteen. Raymond King, fifteen, lured from an employment centre with a promise of work. Sigrun Arnd, eighteen, a student visiting from Germany. Terri Lyn Carson, fifteen, strangled and left in the woods along the Fraser River. Louise Chartrand, seventeen, buried in a shallow grave near Whistler. The children were raped, beaten, bludgeoned.

Eleven children killed in less than seven months. Olson knew how to charm, promise jobs, offer a ride. He preyed on weakness, exploited trust.

It was easy, at first, for police to ignore the crimes, to tell the parents that their children had run away and would probably show up.

That changed with Olson's fourth victim, nine-year-old Simon Partington. Nine-year-olds don't just run away and vanish.

But as parents kept their children close to home and headlines warned of a predator on the loose, police failed to come to grips with the menace. Olson roamed throughout the Lower Mainland, one large community, one hunting ground.

But there was a patchwork of police forces—municipal, RCMP—that didn't communicate with each other. They failed to act on reports of missing children. Olson showed up on suspect lists in different police departments, but they didn't share the information. RCMP officers were transferred in and out, and the case fell through the cracks.

Even when police knew Olson was a prime suspect, delays in setting up surveillance allowed him to kill his last three victims.

Finally, on August 12, their surveillance paid off. Olson was arrested near Port Alberni on Vancouver Island with two female hitchhikers in his car.

Once arrested, Olson used the system to inflict pain on the victims' families, their communities, the courts. On anyone he could hurt, or taunt.

It started with his trial. He pleaded not guilty. Three days after the trial began on January 11, 1982, he changed his plea to guilty. He had struck a deal. He would guide police to the bodies they had not yet discovered and provide details about the other crimes—if they paid $10,000 per killing, with the money going to his wife.

Police, prosecutors, and British Columbia Attorney General agreed. Olson revelled in the experience of guiding officers to the bodies, describing each one in gleeful detail. He collected $100,000. He was sentenced to life in prison.

Public outrage over the "cash for bodies" deal just brought him more attention.

Olson's manipulations to win attention, inflict pain, and taunt the families of his victims and the public had just begun.

Once in prison, Olson toyed with police, claiming to have information on dozens of additional murders. He wrote letters detailing the killings to the families of victims and to politicians until the prison system began censoring his outgoing mail. He told anyone who would listen that he was writing his memoir, with detailed descriptions of the eleven murders, plus scores of other killings and sexual assaults.

He filed a string of lawsuits from inside his special cell, with its wall of Plexiglas in front of the bars to prevent other prisoners from attacking him.

And as soon as Olson was eligible for parole, he applied. He knew there was no chance of success; it was an opportunity to taunt the families and regain the spotlight at his public parole hearing.

No opportunity was missed. When he began receiving the old-age pension, he shared the news with a *Toronto Sun* reporter. He knew the news coverage would outrage the public and wanted the attention.

Clifford Olson died of cancer at seventy-one, in September 2011. No one mourned.

FORGIVENESS

O ne punch, four kicks to the head, and a lawyer lies dying on a bedroom floor as a rowdy house party goes on around him.

His wife and twin four-year-olds wait in a house down the street. But Bob McIntosh isn't coming home to rejoin the New Year's Eve celebrations.

Nothing good, surely, could be expected to come from that grim last night of 1997. But it did.

* * *

Bob and Katy McIntosh had moved to Squamish from Vancouver. He was a successful lawyer and, at forty, a world-class triathlete. She taught at a college, worked with local entrepreneurs, and raised the twins. She was attractive and stylish.

They had a beautiful home on Thunderbird Ridge with spectacular views, lots of friends, and active lives. It was, Katy recalls, a charmed life.

So they had lots to celebrate that New Year's Eve. Friends were visiting with their children. They made a bouillabaisse and looked forward to seeing in the New Year.

When another couple arrived, they mentioned a party at the Cudmore house down the street. Dr. Richard Cudmore was a neighbour and close friend. He had asked McIntosh to keep an eye on his house while he honeymooned in Mexico. McIntosh and the two men decided to check it out. He grabbed a beer, thinking he might fit in better.

Cudmore, it turned out, was right to be nervous.

Light and loud music poured into the street from the Cudmore house. A drunken New Year's Eve party was in full swing, with some 150 young people jammed into the house. Cudmore's nineteen-year-old son, Jamie, had thrown out the invitation, then left his own party.

Jamie, six foot six and powerful, had been picking up money as a collector for local drug dealers. The party attracted some tough people from that world. (Jamie, after a couple of assault convictions, turned his life around and became a stalwart of Canada's national rugby team and a European pro.)

McIntosh and the two friends decided to go in and try to find out what was going on. They quickly became separated. McIntosh headed for the master bedroom, where a group of young people had congregated.

What happened next took seconds. Someone bumped into McIntosh, and he bumped into Ryan MacMillan, a big, drunk twenty-year-old logger with a record for petty crimes. He threw one punch, McIntosh slumped to the floor, and MacMillan left the bedroom without a backward glance.

Then Ryan Aldridge, nineteen, stepped forward and kicked McIntosh. Four full, swinging kicks to the head.

* * *

Katy knew nothing, until the doorbell rang and a friend said Bob was hurt. A police car was waiting. The ten-minute ride to the Squamish Hospital emergency room seemed to take forever.

She rushed into the ER, where one of Bob's running friends was administering CPR. It is like that in towns of 14,000 people. Lives overlap.

It was too late. Bob was dead.

Katy called close friends and family from the hospital, then went home to wait for the twins to wake up. "All I could think about was Sam and Emma, how they had two hours of innocence left," she recalled. "I watched them sleeping and thought, I hope they don't wake up till noon."

And she decided the killing could not be allowed to become a nightmare that hung over their family. "I promised them and I promised myself that underneath the horror of what had just happened we would find a gift."

* * *

Police started investigating. MacMillan soon admitted punching McIntosh. Five days after the killing, he was charged with manslaughter.

But the case was weak. Autopsy results indicated that a punch didn't kill McIntosh.

And the police investigation ran into a wall of silence. Eight to twelve young people were in the bedroom and witnessed the killing; scores more had information that could have helped police.

No one would talk. The people at the party, their friends, maybe even parents, chose to remain silent. They placed protecting one of their own—not being a rat—above bringing a killer to justice.

In September, the Crown stayed the charges against MacMillan. There wasn't enough evidence to make the case.

Squamish kept its secrets.

* * *

Bob's memorial service in the civic centre was attended by about 750 people. Friends, even strangers, wore blue ribbons—the colour of Bob's eyes—to show support. Katy delivered the eulogy.

But life in Squamish was difficult. Family friends didn't know what to say, or burst into tears when they met Katy on the street.

And as days and weeks went by without any progress in the case, Katy had to wonder if each person she passed knew who killed Bob. Once outgoing, enthusiastic, friendly, she now found meeting people exhausting, and groups of teens threatening.

In April, Katy moved to Victoria, where she grew up and where her mother and two brothers still lived. She decided to sue MacMillan and the Cudmores for her husband's death, a decision that angered some in Squamish.

A moustached, grey-haired Victoria lawyer, Mike Hutchison, was handling her lawsuit. By late summer, they were engaged.

It surprised many people. But Katy had a made a quick decision. She was not going to let her life—and her children's—be defined by Bob's death. She could see the temptations to embrace anger, hatred, or self-pity, to give up. She was determined to live every minute fully, as Bob had done.

And she believed that something good could come from the worst day of her life.

* * *

It took four years, but the wall of silence developed cracks. An eight-month RCMP undercover operation that started in late 2001 led to Aldridge, and the undercover officers elicited an admission of guilt in a Richmond hotel room.

But they wanted stronger evidence, and by June 2002, they were ready to bring Aldridge in to try and get a videotaped confession.

Katy Hutchison, who had stayed in close touch with the investigation, had a bold idea. She wanted to talk to Aldridge, to make a personal appeal. Confession, she believed, was important for him. And even more, a guilty plea was needed to spare the twins—now nine—the ordeal of a highly publicized trial.

The RCMP said no. But they let Katy make a videotape. She spoke directly to Aldridge, told him about Bob, and the twins, and how their life had changed since that New Year's Eve. She said they were linked forever, her family and Aldridge. She asked him just to tell the truth.

When the RCMP played the video and showed him pictures of the twins playing with Bob, Aldridge broke down in tears. He confessed.

Then he surprised officers. Could he speak with Katy?

For police, it was a chance to gather more evidence. For Katy Hutchison, it was much more. The next morning, June 21, the RCMP arranged a helicopter flight from Victoria to Squamish, where Katy walked into a bleak, tiny interview room to come face to face with the man who had killed her husband.

"He started to cry as soon as he got in the room. I said, 'It's going to be okay.' As he sobbed it was all I could do not to hold him. Second to the day I gave birth, it was probably the most human moment of my life."

Aldridge apologized, told Katy about his years of nightmares about the night. He gave her letters he had written, one for her and one for the twins. When she left the room, she could see him, sitting alone, sobbing.

"I wanted to make it okay for him. He seemed genuinely remorseful."

Aldridge pleaded guilty to manslaughter and was sentenced to five years in prison. Katy Hutchison was in court, and read a victim impact statement that brought many to tears.

But their relationship was just beginning.

Katy—initially a nervous public speaker—decided to do a couple of presentations in local high schools to tell her story and encourage kids to think about responsibility and the risks of drunken parties and bad choices.

She showed pictures of Bob competing in triathlons, reading to the twins, goofing around with his friends, and talked about their lives.

And then Katy showed a photo of him lying on the table in the morgue.

It was powerful. But just a start.

In 2003, an article on restorative justice, on bringing offenders and victims together to help both heal, captured her imagination. After much preparation, Katy met with Ryan for five hours in the Matsqui federal penitentiary, showed him her presentation. They talked about Bob, the children, Ryan's family, and life behind bars. And as the time came to leave, she reached out to the man who killed her husband.

"I do not know what your plans are after you are released from prison, but if you would like to come and work with me in the schools, I would be honoured to work with you."

Their first two presentations were inside prisons, but then Aldridge and Hutchison shared their stories together in schools and community groups.

"We cannot change the fact that our lives came crashing together on New Year's Eve in 1997," she wrote in *Walking After Midnight*, her frank account of the experience. "Ryan and I came at this journey from opposite directions. We met somewhere in the middle and chose to walk forward side by side."

"It is simply the best we can do."

WHOSE BODY IS THIS?

S ue Rodriguez walked out of the doctor's office in August 1991 and knew everything in her life had changed.

She was forty-one, mother of a son just starting school. She had begun working as a legal secretary, was happily married, and had a home in the pastoral Saanich Peninsula outside Victoria.

And, Rodriguez had just learned, she was dying.

She had noticed numbness and weakness in her left hand in April, and been to several doctors seeking answers.

Now she knew. She had amyotrophic lateral sclerosis—Lou Gehrig's disease.

Rodriguez could expect to live two to three years after the onset of the disease—the time she first noticed the numbness in her hand.

As ALS progressed, nerve cells in her brain and spinal cord would die. They control all the muscles in the body. As the cells died, her muscles would weaken and atrophy.

People with ALS lose the ability to walk, or use their arms. The muscles of the head and neck waste away, so they can't speak, chew, or swallow. They must be fed, first by someone else, then, as swallowing becomes impossible, through a tube. They are at risk of respiratory infections and choking.

As their conditions worsen, people are likely to be paralyzed, unable to lift their heads. Machines keep them breathing through tubes. Caregivers, family or paid, empty catheters and clean bowel movements and try to prevent bedsores.

Death usually comes because patients choke to death on food, develop pneumonia, or suffocate when their muscles used in breathing no longer work.

And through it all, patients' brains are otherwise unaffected—they feel pain, are aware of their circumstances. The mind is a prisoner in a wasting body.

Rodriguez knew that was not for her.

She researched the disease, decided she would not die that way.

"I'm not afraid of death at all," Rodriguez told Anne Mullins of the *Vancouver Sun*. "But I fear gasping for breath, panicking, being in a situation where I am hooked up to a respirator, unable to swallow, unable to move, unable to do anything for myself."

"I hate to be entertaining the thought, but I will do what I have to do in order to die in as peaceful a manner as possible."

The law, Rodriguez found, made dying peacefully, on her terms, extremely difficult. Suicide is legal in Canada. But helping someone else commit suicide is a criminal offence.

Rodriguez wanted as much time with her husband and young son as possible. By the time she decided to end her life, she would likely be physically unable to make it happen. She would need help.

She knew she couldn't ask her husband to help end her life when the time came. It would be too difficult emotionally. And he would be breaking the law. If he went to jail, who would care for their son?

So Rodriguez decided to do everything she could to change the law. If not in time for her, then for others.

It was a brave choice. Polls indicated most Canadians supported an individual's right to choose the time of his or her death and to be assisted by a doctor.

But powerful groups opposed any change, and politicians shied away from the issue.

Rodriguez went public with her illness, and her desire to end her life when she chose, in the way she chose.

She launched a legal challenge to the law barring assisted

suicide, arguing that it was discriminatory and violated her constitutional rights.

Other Canadians, she noted, had the legal right to end their lives. Because the progression of her illness meant she would be incapacitated, and assisted suicide was illegal, she did not.

While the challenge made its way through the courts, on an inevitable path to the Supreme Court of Canada, Rodriguez sacrificed her personal privacy to lobby for changes to the Criminal Code.

All the time, the clock was ticking.

Two months after she went public, Rodriguez urged a parliamentary committee to help change the law. She was already too sick to travel to Ottawa. Her powerful video presentation had to speak for her.

Rodriguez filmed the presentation in her family room, perched on a black leather couch, the sun dappling the treed garden outside her window. Her voice was already affected by the deterioration of her muscles—she spoke slowly, with little affect. She was gaunt, her dark hair cut short on the sides and swept back.

Her words, though, were powerful.

"My name is Sue Rodriguez. A year ago, when I was first diagnosed, I was quite agile. Today I can barely walk.

"I had full control of my hands except for some occasional twitching. Today, as you can see, my hands are misshapen and it is all I can do to sign my name in a scrawl.

"There's much worse to come.... Soon I will be unable to walk. I will be unable to breathe without a respirator. I will be unable to eat or swallow—unable to move without assistance.

"I want to ask you, gentlemen, if I cannot give consent to my own death, then whose body is this? Who owns my life?"

Compelling. But MPs did not want to touch the polarizing issue. Liberal MP John Nunziata even fought to keep the video from being seen by the committee, saying that if Rodriguez was too sick to appear, she should submit a written brief, though she was also unable to write by that point. An anti-assisted suicide group linked changing the law to the death camps of Nazi Germany.

The politicians wouldn't act. Her only choice was the courts.

The British Columbia Supreme Court ruled against Rodriguez on December 29, saying assisted suicide was not a right protected under the Charter of Rights and Freedoms.

On March 8, 1993, the British Columbia Court of Appeal also ruled against Rodriguez, in a split decision. Two justices said that the rights of Rodriguez were not being affected, and that it was up to Parliament to decide if the law should be changed.

But Chief Justice Allan McEachern said Rodriguez's fundamental Charter rights were being violated, because they prevented a doctor from helping her end her life when suffering became unbearable.

That left the Supreme Court of Canada. But on September 30, the court rejected her bid to overturn the law in a 5-4 decision. The majority ruled there is no Charter right to assisted suicide, and that the law expressed society's rejection of suicide and fear of abuses if the law was changed.

The four dissenting justices said Rodriguez's rights were being violated. Other Canadians could legally choose when to end their lives. The law against assisted suicide denied her that right. And she was being made to suffer because of possible abuses that had nothing to do with her.

Rodriguez saw a glimmer of hope, at least for others.

"While I may not benefit from the decision today, I hope that Parliament will act and allow those who are in my situation to benefit in the future," she whispered from her wheelchair. "It has been worth it, far more than I ever anticipated. People are talking about this and thinking about these issues."

But she had never been counting on the courts. Seven months earlier, she had found a doctor—Dr. X—willing to help her end her suffering when she decided the time was right. In mid-January, she set a date. She could no longer hold her son, and did not want him to have to see her suffer and waste away.

On February 11, 1994, just under three years since her diagnosis, Sue Rodriguez had a last dinner with her husband,

Henry, and son, Cole. The next morning, they left the home for the day.

New Democrat MP Svend Robinson, a friend and an advocate for her right to die, arrived at her house that morning. Rodriguez had asked him to be with her. They talked, and she gave him a list of friends and family to call.

Dr. X arrived, willing to break the law to help Rodriguez decide when it was time to die.

"Sue remained serene and calm throughout and in total control," Robinson said. "She faced her death with incredible courage and dignity. I held her in my arms. She peacefully lapsed into unconsciousness and stopped breathing approximately two hours later. The doctor then left."

Robinson said he called a palliative-care physician shortly after Dr. X left, and soon after made calls to the RCMP and coroner's service.

An autopsy found she had died of overdoses of a sedative and morphine. The RCMP took a brief interest in trying to identify Dr. X, but there were no charges.

But Rodriguez's hope that her death would lead to a public debate about assisted suicide and changes to the law was misplaced. Twenty years after her death, the laws remain unchanged.

SMUGGLERS AND DEATH

The west coast was a wild place in 1864, and not just because of the waves crashing on the rocky shores.

The gold rush was bringing another wave of newcomers into the colonies of Vancouver Island and British Columbia. Conflicts with Natives were increasing, with each side blaming the other for indignities and attacks. Traders from the colonies and the United States sailed up and down the coast, flouting the ban on selling alcohol to Natives imposed by Governor James Douglas six years earlier.

The Royal Navy, already with too few ships to patrol the coast, was on alert over warnings that Confederate forces in the American Civil War planned pirate-style raids on shipping and faced a simmering boundary dispute with the United States.

It was a tense time for the navy's Pacific Station commander, Rear Admiral Joseph Denman, who had earned a reputation for aggressive leadership in his battles against slavers in West Africa. (Denman Island, off Fanny Bay on Vancouver Island, is named for him.)

Land-based policing was scant and improvised. The Colony of Vancouver Island, created thirteen years earlier, had a police commissioner, but policing authority was delegated to local magistrates, most with no qualifications.

William Duncan was one of those magistrates. Duncan was an ambitious British missionary who had established a utopian Christian community with members of the Tsimshian First Nation two years earlier. Metlakahtla was about ten kilometres from Prince Rupert and held up as a model; Duncan was a celebrity in the mission world.

His community plan included law and order, and Duncan had appointed ten Tsimshian men as police officers. When colonial officials reported suspicions that the fifteen-ton American sloop *Random* was illegally selling alcohol in coastal communities near Port Simpson, Duncan acted.

He authorized the arrest of the captain and seizure of the ship and cargo. On August 17, he dispatched five Native constables, by canoe, to seize the sloop.

It was a risky mission. The officers had to paddle toward Port Simpson, about thirty-five kilometres away, to find the *Random*.

Tensions were already running high between traders and Natives after a series of confrontations, some violent. Racism was a given; Natives were seen as savages. White sailors were not going to accept orders or take direction from Natives, even Native police officers.

The Tsimshian constables paddled through the day and into the night before they found the *Random*. The crew wouldn't let them board until dawn, but once they were aboard things seemed to go well. The crew agreed to sail to Metlakahtla to deal with the charges, and one of the constables set out to tell Duncan they were on their way.

But resentment—fuelled by consumption of the ship's cargo of whisky—set in as the day went on. An argument broke out, and the three-man American crew said they weren't going to Metlakahtla, but planned to flee the twenty-five kilometres to Russian territory (the current Alaska).

When the four remaining constables objected, the crew took up guns and started firing. It was chaos on the sloop. One constable was wounded in the hip, two others in their arms. They managed to scramble into a canoe and escape to Dundas Island.

But Cst. Reuben Onslow, a thirty-one-year-old member of the force, was fatally shot and disappeared into the Pacific. (His Aboriginal name was either Cowallah or Cowaltah. Both spellings appeared in records.)

When word reached Victoria days later, Denman sent HMS *Grappler* to look for the Americans. But the thirty-two-metre gunboat, built for the Crimean War, had little chance of success. Under full steam, the journey from the naval base at Esquimalt to the scene of the crime took more than three days.

The colonial government posted a $250 reward for anyone who shared information or brought in the three crew members, a sizeable sum in 1864 even during a gold rush. Colonial officials enlisted Russian and American help to find the *Random* and its rogue crew.

U.S. officers stationed on San Juan Island, about thirty kilometres from Victoria, seized the sloop at anchor at nearby Orcas Island. But the three crew members escaped into the bush and were never apprehended.

"I am not much surprised at this," Frederick Seymour, the newly appointed governor of the Colony of British Columbia reported in a dispatch to London. "The feeling of the majority of the population in the adjoining territory would be strongly opposed to the surrendering to British justice [of] American citizens who had merely shot Indians who were interfering, (though on behalf of the law) with the traffic carried on by the white men."

Seymour reported to Edward Cardwell, the British secretary of state for colonies, that he had accepted Duncan's proposals on measures "to pacify the Indians at Metlakahtla." A surgeon and nurses were sent up to care for the wounded men, and Onslow's widow received twenty pounds compensation.

And the incident was forgotten for almost 150 years — until 2002, when a Victoria Police Department constable with an interest in history stumbled on an account of the crime. Jonathan Sheldan dug into the case, checking old newspapers and reports. With help, he learned the details.

And he realized Cst. Reuben (Cowallah/Cowaltah) Onslow was the first Native police officer to be killed in the line of duty in what was to become British Columbia, and perhaps in Canada.

In 2007, Onslow's name was carved into the monument to fallen peace officers outside the legislative building in Victoria.

STEALING THE WORLD

Gilbert Bland was well named. He was forgettable. Average. Mid-forties, about five feet nine inches, 160 to 170 pounds, with a moustache and sandy-coloured hair, reddish in some lights.

He dressed in the slightly rumpled uniform of the invisible middle-aged man—khaki slacks, a tweed jacket or blazer, dress shirt.

And with a briefcase, a razor blade, and a vaguely reassuring air, he robbed libraries, museums, and archives across North America of priceless treasures.

He didn't need a gun. Just a polite smile, and nerve. And collectors who didn't ask too many questions when Bland offered them that prized rare map they had been hunting.

Bland had a bumpy life, with a series of early run-ins with the law. After an elaborate scam to create a bunch of fake identities and claim unemployment benefits landed him in a federal prison in Oklahoma, it looked like he was going legit. He and his wife started a company, and Bland made it through the 1980s without getting into more trouble.

Then, one day in the early '90s, Bland bid on the contents of an abandoned storage locker, hoping to find something of value to sell. Sorting through someone's forgotten treasures, he came across a stash of old maps. And he quickly learned they could be worth real money.

Bland and his wife needed money. Their business was failing, and they had big debts and little income. Bland was forty-six, young enough to start again.

Maybe maps were the answer.

And in 1994, they moved to Coral Springs, Florida, and opened Antique Maps and Collectibles in a strip mall. It was an unlikely location, but that didn't matter. Bland did business over the Internet, sending out lists of maps for sale and taking inquiries from collectors.

His timing was good. Map collectors had always been fervent, obsessive even. But soaring values brought new buyers, almost as keen and a lot less knowledgeable.

Still, Bland was a newcomer, with few connections and little experience. A few collectors who talked to him were surprised that he didn't seem to know that much about maps. His prices were too low.

But he had an inexplicable ability to get his hands on specific antique maps as soon as people asked him about them.

Bland had found a shortcut, and a great way to increase profit. He just stole the maps he needed.

That's how he came to the door of the British Columbia Archives on October 5, 1995, a greyish fall day. The archives, beside the Royal British Columbia Museum and across the street from Rattenbury's grey stone legislative building, welcomed researchers.

Bland signed in under the alias of James Perry, and signed out nine rare books to use in his "research."

And as he leafed through them, he paused at particularly marketable maps and sliced them out, sliding twenty into his briefcase. He walked out with one of the earliest maps of the Pacific Rim and pages from a 1601 edition of *Theatrum Orbis Terrarum*, the first world atlas.

The maps were a dealer's bread and butter. Rare and desirable, but not so rare that too many questions would be asked. Maps from the *Theatrum*, for example, would likely retail at $500 to $1,000. Bland's haul would bring him $10,000 to $20,000 for a few hours' work.

The next day Bland paid a visit to the University of British Columbia Library's special collections, and left with another nineteen maps.

The institutions—like many before them—didn't even know they had been robbed.

Libraries and archives were easy pickings. Staff were trusting, and the institutions hadn't recognized that the soaring value of maps would attract criminals. A 1482 edition of Ptolemy's map book *Geographia* could be bought for $5,000 in 1950. In 2009, a copy sold for more than $1 million.

When Bland was caught, it was by a library user, not staff. She spotted him in Baltimore's spectacular George Peabody Library on December 7, 1995, two months after his British Columbia visit.

Bland was acting oddly. The researcher wasn't sure, but she thought she saw him take a map from an old book. She alerted library staff as Bland left the library. There was a bizarre half-walking, half-jogging chase. Library security staff weren't really sure about tackling a middle-aged researcher. Bland tossed a notebook into some bushes before the guards persuaded him to return to the library.

When they checked the notebook, staff found three maps—more than two centuries old—tucked into the pages.

Bland was smooth. He apologized, offered to pay the library $700 cash, on the spot, for damaging the book. They accepted the offer. No one called police.

It was a huge mistake. When the library's security director took time to go through the notebook, he found a shopping list—Bland had written down desirable maps, and the institutions where he could steal them.

But the Peabody quickly redeemed itself, alerting other institutions to Bland's agenda and pseudonym. Ultimately, nineteen libraries and archives found they had been visited by Bland, as James Perry. When they checked the books he had signed out, maps were missing.

The British Columbia Archives and the University of British Columbia were among the victims.

"I got physically ill," recalled Gary Mitchell, then the deputy provincial archivist. "For my colleagues and I, it was just awful. It felt like we had suffered a death in the family."

Bland had come and gone without a trace. "No one noticed him at all," Mitchell said. "No one recalls him."

It was the same at all the other libraries.

Bland knew he was busted, that the FBI would soon be on his trail.

He didn't panic. He planned. He emptied the Florida store, locked the door, and left a hand-lettered note saying it was closed. He hid his trove of stolen maps. They were, he realized, his best bargaining chip. And he judged, rightly, that prosecutors would not know what to make of his thefts, and juries might not think the crimes serious.

On January 2, 1996, a month after his bad luck in Baltimore, Bland's preparations were complete. He turned himself in.

Bland and his lawyer offered the prosecutors a deal. Accept a plea bargain, and a short jail sentence, and Bland would tell them how to get the stolen maps—or some of them—back. Or take a chance on trials and losing the maps forever.

It worked. Bland pleaded guilty and pointed police to a Florida storage locker with 150 maps, then told them where to find additional maps that he had already sold to other dealers.

The British Columbia Archives flew an expert down to the FBI lab in Quantico, Virginia, and recovered 18 of its 20 stolen maps. UBC, unhappily, did less well, retrieving only five of 19 stolen maps.

And Bland—the man no one could remember—served less than seventeen months in jail and was free once again.

HOCKEY NIGHT

Roy Spencer scrimped and sacrificed to push his twin sons, Brian and Byron, toward the NHL. He stood outside night after night in the bitter cold and flooded a rink outside their log cabin in Fort St. John. He taught them the game, drilled them at the dinner table.

But when the moment came—when Brian made the big time—things went terribly, fatally wrong.

Fort St. John was a hard town, the kind of place that turns out tough hockey players who make it to the pros. It was an eighteen-hour drive to Vancouver, and the town of 7,000 was farther north than parts of Alaska. The winters were long and cold.

And Roy Spencer was a hard man. He was a mechanic who worked hard, drank hard, and pushed his sons hard.

In 1949, when Brian and Byron were born, northern British Columbia was still the frontier, a place where most people made their own way and weren't much keen on being told what to do.

Roy Spencer was one of those people. And he pushed the same values on his boys.

Brian took to the pressure. He excelled at hockey, and showed some of his father's aptitude for both drinking and toughness.

Toughness was important. In 1970, there were fourteen NHL teams, and about 160 jobs for forwards like Brian Spencer. There were 15,000 kids playing minor hockey in British Columbia alone, most with at least vague dreams of the NHL. Scouts wanted to see players willing to endure anything to win.

Brian, after his father's schooling, had a chance. At sixteen, he left home—and quit school—to play for the Estevan Bruins in Saskatchewan. Over the next three years, he played in Calgary, Regina, back in Estevan, and then with the Swift Current Broncos. No one considered it strange that a teen, far from home, could be called into the rink and be told he had been traded and needed to get on the Greyhound to meet his new owners.

Spencer didn't care. He was driven. And back home, his dad was watching, counting on him.

He figured out how to get noticed. In his last year in junior, he racked up almost a point a game and got even tougher, tripling the amount of time he spent in the penalty box.

"Spinner," they called him, because of his frenetic, crashing play. The nickname stuck. A good-looking, tough kid.

It worked. Scouts for the Toronto Maple Leafs took notice, and Spencer was the fifty-fifth player picked in the draft. Not a top prospect—only eighty-five players were drafted. But it meant the Leafs wanted him. Those hours in the backyard rink with frozen toes, the long bus rides across the Prairies, all that pressure from his dad. All worth it.

Spencer couldn't stick with the Maple Leafs in his first training camp in 1969, and was sent down to the Tulsa Oilers, a farm team in the rough Central League. He scored thirteen goals, and spent 186 minutes in the penalty box—the most on the team. He didn't back down from fights, even if at under six feet, some 180 pounds, he was small for a fighter.

His father was proud, but still pushing Brian to try harder, make the NHL.

And Brian got the call in December 1970. Get to Toronto. You'll be playing for the Maple Leafs. Darryl Sittler, Bobby Baun, Paul Henderson, Jacques Plante, Dave Keon. And Brian Spencer.

It was a great week. Spencer played well in the Leafs' 4-0 win over rival Montreal on Wednesday. On Thursday, he learned his wife had given birth to a daughter in Tulsa.

And his dad was going to get a chance to watch him play on *Hockey Night in Canada* on Saturday night. Spencer had even been chosen to be the sweaty player interviewed between periods by the CBC.

Roy Spencer got ready. He bought a new television antenna to make sure he pulled in the signal from the CBC station in Prince George. He invited friends to come over, laid in party supplies. The Leafs versus the Chicago Blackhawks. His boy facing off against superstar Bobby Hull. It was the dream.

Almost. The Vancouver Canucks had joined the NHL that year. CBC brass decided to broadcast the hapless Canucks versus the Oakland Golden Seals, a team distinguished by their white skates, in British Columbia.

Roy Spencer exploded when he got the news. He phoned the Prince George CBC station and yelled at a news staffer, threatening to come to the station.

And he did. Grabbing a couple of guns—and, according to some accounts, a bottle of rye whiskey—he set out on the two-hour drive to Prince George.

Around 7:30 p.m., Spencer pulled into the dark parking lot and encountered news anchor Tim Haertel. He stuck his 9mm handgun in Haertel's back. It looked "50 feet around" to the newsman. "He had the hammer pulled back and he said he was going to use it."

Things just got worse. Spencer ended up with eight staff lined up at gunpoint. "I don't want to kill anybody. I've killed before."

"If I can't watch my son play hockey tonight, nobody gets to watch hockey tonight."

Spencer was "cold sober, but shaking like a leaf," said program director Dan Prentice. When Spencer told him to take the station off the air, he did.

The CBC went dark across northern British Columbia.

But a radio station shared the offices. An announcer knew something was wrong and called the RCMP.

When Spencer walked into the parking lot, officers were waiting.

Cpl. Roger Post told him to "Hold it right there."

Spencer fired, wounding another officer in the foot.

And Post and Cst. Steve Lezinski fired four shots. Spencer took two bullets in the chest and one in the head. He was dead on arrival at the hospital.

Brian Spencer got the news early the next morning, in a phone call from his mother. Leafs' boss Jim Gregory asked if he wanted to head home right away.

But the Maple Leafs had a game against Buffalo that day.

"My dad wanted me to be a hockey player more than he wanted anything in the world," he told Gregory. "I think he would want me to play and that's what I'm going to do."

The Leafs won 4-3. Spencer had two assists, fought Buffalo tough guy Tracy Pratt, and was the game's second star.

His dad would have approved. Leafs' coach John McLellan did. "I knew he had the muscle and desire to play in the National Hockey League. Now I know he has the mental toughness and the heart."

But Spencer's career with the Leafs faltered. He spent much of the next year in Tulsa. He moved to the New York Islanders, the Buffalo Sabres, then Pittsburgh. He was a fan favourite, but the nickname "Spinner" increasingly became associated with erratic behaviour off the ice. His career ended in the minors.

Life after hockey was a disaster. Spencer never made big money, and always spent what he had. He moved to Florida, almost broke, certainly bitter, hung around with bad companions, drank and did drugs, living in a trailer and working as a mechanic. In March 1988, he was charged with murdering a client of a girlfriend who worked as a prostitute. He was acquitted.

But three months later, Spencer and a friend were out driving in Riviera Beach. They bought cocaine, and minutes later someone tried to rob them.

Brian Spencer was shot in the chest. He died the next morning, June 3, 1988.

MAYDAY, MAYDAY, MAYDAY

It was supposed to be routine. A milk run to shuttle passengers from Vancouver to Prince George, Fort St. John, Fort Nelson, and Watson Lake and Whitehorse.

The forty-six passengers—including four young children—climbed the ramp and found their seats on Canadian Pacific Airlines Flight 21, welcomed by the steward and two stewardesses.

Capt. Jack Steele, a forty-one-year-old veteran of the Royal Canadian Air Force, headed the three-man crew.

The DC-6B was a shiny four-engine workhorse, with a white, red, and silver paint scheme and Canadian Pacific's stylish script logo painted above the small windows.

They rolled down the runway and off the ground at 2:42 p.m. on July 8, 1965. The first leg to Prince George should have taken about ninety minutes at the plane's 500-km/h cruising speed.

For a few passengers, it was routine. For most, the flight was an adventure. Air travel was new, and passengers dressed up for the occasion.

Helge and Liv Rognerud, from Norway, were part of a group heading to jobs in a Cassiar asbestos mine, their infant son and daughter tucked in beside them. Doris Harris of Halifax was on the last leg of a long trip to Prince George to see her son and his family. H. A. Janssen, regional manager, was heading to Williams Lake to open a new Volkswagen dealership. (The Beetle, at about $1,700, was selling well across Canada.)

The travellers settled in, lit up cigarettes in those days before smoking bans. The plane climbed over the Coast Mountains.

At 3:29 p.m., about forty-seven minutes into the flight, the crew checked in with Vancouver air traffic control. They had passed Ashcroft, flying at 4,900 metres. They would reach Williams Lake about 3:48 p.m. Prince George would only be about 130 kilometres away.

Routine. Less than ten minutes later, Vancouver control called Flight 21 and got no reply.

Two minutes later, there were three cries of "Mayday" from the airplane. Then silence. The plane vanished from the radar.

But 330 kilometres away from Vancouver, witnesses watched in horror. Tom Shaylor was working at a sawmill, idly watching the plane, when things went terribly wrong.

"Then there was this awful blast … a boom and we could see it sort of split apart," he said. The tail was blasted away from the body of the plane. Dark objects spilled from the fuse- lage. It sounded like a dynamite blast, said Shaylor, a Second World War veteran.

The airplane tilted nose down, spun slowly, and crashed into giant pines. It fell so straight down that the wreckage, among splintered trees, looked like a cross from the air.

Slim Sherk, a British Columbia Forest Service pilot, was sent to investigate when a plume of black smoke was reported about forty kilometres west of Williams Lake. Sherk saw the burning plane. He counted at least twenty, maybe forty, bodies scattered on the ground.

Forestry workers and ambulance attendants from 100- Mile House rushed to the scene. But there were no survivors. Bodies, and pieces of bodies, were scattered in the woods. The objects that witnesses saw falling from the plane were passen- gers, sucked out in the seconds after the blast.

The wreckage burned all night. When police and Depart- ment of Transport investigators entered the plane the next day, they found twenty-nine bodies, many still with seat belts fastened.

They were murdered. Investigators knew right away that a bomb had brought down Flight 21.

The evidence was compelling. Paint had been blasted beneath the skin of some passengers. A flight attendant's overnight bag stowed near the rear of the plane was found some 300 metres from the wreckage, and showed signs of having been near an explosion. The RCMP x-rayed the bodies and found a piece of metal that appeared to be from a detonator.

Crash investigators, reconstructing parts of the fallen plane, became convinced there had been a deadly explosion in the left rear lavatory.

But why would anyone want to blow up the plane?

The RCMP, with few leads, decided to do psychological profiles and background checks on all the passengers.

And four names stood out.

Douglas Edgar, a forty-year-old Surrey man, had spent $3.50 to buy $125,000 worth of life insurance less than half an hour before boarding the flight. His wife, daughter, mother, and a niece were the beneficiaries. Buying life insurance was not that suspicious. Companies had vending machines in airports to allow nervous flyers to buy last-minute insurance, with envelopes to mail the policies to their families. But Edgar had told his family he was flying to Prince George because he had been offered a pulp mill job. The Mounties couldn't find any evidence that was true.

Steve Koleszar, of Vancouver, was experienced with explosives, and had been charged with murder seven years earlier. (And acquitted.) But the fifty-four-year-old was on his way to a new job, and had no apparent motive.

Peter Broughton was flying to a summer job in Cassiar. The twenty-nine-year-old was a gun enthusiast, and almost three pounds of gunpowder were missing from his personal inventory. But he had no reason to blow up the DC-6.

And Livingstone King of Toronto worked for an accounting firm that had audited the books of Atlantic Acceptance Corporation. The company had collapsed without warning a month earlier. It was fraud, the worst in Canadian history, and many investors lost everything. A federal royal commission was ultimately appointed to investigate the mess.

Not suspects, the police were quick to say. They just had unanswered questions about them.

There were other rumours. A strange man had been seen leaving the rear lavatory before takeoff in Vancouver. A flight attendant had smuggled explosives onto the plane as a favour to her boyfriend. A miner was preparing charges in the washroom when one went off accidentally. In 1965, there was no security or searches. You showed your ticket, checked your bag, and walked on board.

But police could never answer the main questions—who brought the explosives onto the aircraft, and why.

Most of the wreckage is still in the forests where the plane crashed more than a half century ago, trees growing up around the plane.

But it gives up no answers. The crash of Canadian Pacific Airlines Flight 21 remains a mystery. Someone killed fifty-two people.

And we don't know why.

GO HOME!

When the first ship came in the summer of 1999, British Columbians were intrigued, even sympathetic. It was like aliens from another planet, seeking a haven in Canada. No one talked about criminals.

The rusty hulk intercepted off Vancouver Island's Gold River on July 20 was carrying 123 Chinese migrants. They had braved a thirty-eight-day journey in horrific conditions for a chance at life in North America.

The first news reports presented a gripping tale of suffering in a filthy ship, sleeping on plywood boards, hungry and sick, with a scant supply of bad water, all to start a new life.

It was a heroic feat of endurance. "Think of your worst nightmare on a ship and that's what you got," said a Coast Guard officer.

For a few days, there was even warmth for the 106 men and seventeen women—including ten minors—so keen to start anew, like millions of immigrants before them.

Less than two months later, three more ships had arrived and the mood in Canada was poisonous. The ships had brought just 599 migrants. Every ten days that year, the same number of people arrived in Canada by air or road and sought refugee status. No one was much concerned about them.

But politicians, media, and much of the public were outraged or frightened by a few hundred desperate people on rusty ships. They were queue jumpers, criminals, maybe even diseased, the reports suggested.

The migrants had committed no criminal offences. They might be ineligible to remain in Canada, but they weren't illegal. The only possible criminals, under Canadian law, were the organizers. It was a remarkable case of collective hysteria.

There was little hint of any of that in the days after the first boat arrived.

The migrants were detained and held for immigration hearings in a gym at CFB Esquimalt, the giant naval base in Victoria.

Eleven were identified as possible paid crew, who might face criminal charges. But the rest were viewed kindly. "They're very calm," a Coast Guard official said. "They're polite to the officers they're dealing with. There's certainly no aggression or anything like that at all. I would guess they're happy to be on ground and in somewhat of a protected state."

But things began to change. News stories raised the cost of housing the migrants. People started to talk about queue-jumping and whether criminals were among the travellers. RCMP officers said they found a weapon fashioned from an aluminum food plate and decided to search the gym. They found pens and combs, and declared them potential weapons. After that, the migrants were handcuffed any time they left the gym.

Except they suddenly weren't migrants any more. The TV news talked about "illegal aliens."

The Chinese arrivals seemed happy to have survived the journey and ready for whatever happened next. They had paid snakeheads varying amounts—$20,000 or more—for the chance to come to North America. An average wage in Fujian province, their home, was six dollars a day. Even with the huge debt, there was a chance to work hard and send money to families.

Immigration laws called for speedy hearings. If migrants asked for refugee status, immigration officials were to decide if they posed a risk or were likely to disappear. By August 4, two-thirds of the migrants had been released to be supported by non-profit agencies or, in the case of minors, into the government's care.

Things calmed down.

Then, barely four weeks later, the second boat came. Canadian Forces patrol planes spotted an unmarked cargo ship about 240 kilometres off the wild Queen Charlotte Islands. The government dispatched a small armada—planes, three Coast Guard ships, and an RCMP ship.

The crew eluded the pursuers and made a dash for the coast. They dumped 131 Chinese migrants—including forty-three minors as young as eleven—in a shallow, forbidding bay on Kunghit Island, where they shivered on a rocky beach until they were rescued. Goetz Hanisch, who owned a lodge on the island, transported two men and a woman. "They're cold, they seem hungry, one's sick and holding his stomach all the time and they're crying," he reported.

The crew made a run for it. But the aging ship couldn't escape the air force surveillances. The RCMP boarded the ship in international waters, arrested the eight crew, and headed for shore.

It was only 254 people so far. Less than a planeload. But the friendly, welcoming face of Canada got uglier, and crazier. Media coverage focused on the perils. A flotilla of coming ships was predicted.

The *Victoria Times Colonist* polled its readers—unscientifically—and found ninety-seven percent favoured sending the migrants home without hearings. The newspaper ran a giant GO HOME headline on its front page.

Politicians joined in. Canada's Immigration Minister, Elinor Caplan, said she was looking at tougher laws "in light of these troubling incidents." Reform party leader Preston Manning thought Parliament should be recalled to respond to the emergency by suspending the Charter of Rights.

It was a crazy time. The eight crew members from the second ship turned out to be Korean. Before their first appearance in a Victoria courtroom, Judge Jeanne Harvey ordered that no one be allowed in without protective breathing masks. Reporters, greeted by a locked door, rushed to a nearby dentist's office to get some surgical masks.

The Koreans shuffled into court in their green prison coveralls. They faced a roomful of people wearing everything from cheap, disposable white masks to elaborate, military-style gas masks. The translator had a purple mask with two breathing tubes snaking down like tentacles. Unfortunately, it made her difficult to understand in either language.

It was unnecessary and irrational. The crew was healthy. They were not in quarantine, and came to the hearing in a van with Mounties who saw no need for masks.

Not all the migrants were unwelcome. A well-fed dog was on the second boat, a Labrador crossbreed that the Victoria SPCA named Breeze. Adoption offers came in from across Canada.

The migrants on the second boat weren't as well briefed. Asked why they came to Canada, seventy-seven of the 131 said they wanted to make money. The correct answer is as a refugee fleeing persecution.

This was all getting expensive. Immigration Canada spent about $400,000 in two weeks dealing with the new arrivals. The provincial government had to find space for about fifty children in government care.

Partly, costs were so high because of the push to "get tough" with the migrants. Refugee claimants are usually released and told when to appear for a hearing. Almost three-quarters of the adults on the first boat were released into the community.

But all the adults on the second boat were detained, an expensive alternative. (It is worth noting that almost half the adults on the first boat who were released disappeared before their refugee hearings.)

Then came ship number three. A Canadian Forces Aurora patrol plane spotted it on August 30. It looked like it was about to sink, so the navy and coast guard boarded the next morning and took the people to safety. Another 163 adults and twenty-seven minors entered the system. The migrants were ferried to Gold River, a town on Vancouver Island's west coast hammered by a mill closure and job losses.

Ten days later, the fourth ship, the largest yet, arrived. The captain tried briefly to outrun a Canadian Forces destroyer, then hoisted a white T-shirt as a flag of surrender. There were 146 people on board.

The summer had brought 599 people to Canada's shores in two months—about 2.4 percent of the total who would make claims for asylum that year.

But somehow, the boat people sparked fear and anger, while the 24,000 refugee claimants coming by air or land were ignored.

Everyone braced for another wave of migrant ships on the British Columbia coast. Government departments worked on contingency plans.

But the ships never came. The botched journeys might have made people unwilling to book passage on the route, or the snakeheads might have found a better way to help people travel to North America. Maybe there were more jobs in China.

In British Columbia, 250 migrants were still in jail, taking up about ten percent of the available beds. An old prison in Prince George was reopened especially for the migrants.

The refugee process was painfully slow. By the next spring, there had been two mass deportations of ninety people each time. There had been an unsuccessful jail escape, a small prison riot, and an eight-day hunger strike by female inmates.

*   *   *

Of the 599 people on the four boats, 580 made refugee claims and only twenty-four were accepted.

But only 330 people were deported.

Most of the rest just disappeared. The detained teenagers, in the province's care, flew away like birds leaving the nest—twenty-five in one night in Victoria. They had sacrificed too much to be sent back to China. Adults released from detention did the same. It was a good deal for taxpayers—the costs stopped once they had checked out of the system.

And no actual kingpins or organizers were ever charged with a crime. In fact, from all four ships, only five people were convicted of "organizing, aiding or abetting the coming into Canada of a group of persons who were not in possession of valid travel documents."

The whole exercise cost, based on the lowest estimates, $40 million—or $67,000 per migrant. Much more than they paid for the journey.

And for one ugly summer, Canadians seemed a meaner people.

SUBURBAN TERRORISTS

The van full of dynamite rolled across the lawn and stopped outside the Litton Systems factory in a Toronto suburb. The driver, Ann Hansen, flicked a switch to start the timer. She stepped out, set down a carboard box with a warning that the van was a rolling bomb, and disappeared into the night. It was 11:15 p.m. on a cloudy Thursday night in 1982, two weeks before Halloween.

From a nearby phone booth, Julie Belmas called the factory, which had been the scene of protests over Litton's work on guidance systems for U.S. cruise missiles. Belmas warned security that the van was a rolling bomb. They had twenty-five minutes to evacuate the building and clear the streets.

The guard didn't understand the message. Nervous and worried about the call being traced, Belmas hung up without answering his questions.

Just fourteen minutes later, a huge explosion rocked the factory, shook homes up to five kilometres away, and sent shrapnel in all directions. Seven people—Litton workers and police—were hurt, two seriously.

Direct Action, an odd collection of Vancouver anarchists who became known as the Squamish Five, had staged their most spectacular terror attack.

But not their first. Or their last.

* * *

They were an unlikely crew. Brent Taylor, twenty-five at the time of the blast, went to Oak Bay High School in Victoria's poshest community, the son of two university professors. He hit the road after high school, first to party, then to learn from U.S. terror groups like the Symbionese Liberation Army, famous for kidnapping Patty Hearst. He told his father he was going to be a revolutionary.

Ann Hansen, twenty-eight, grew up in Concord, a small town later captured by Toronto's northward sprawl. She was one of five children of Danish immigrants who found a better life on an acreage amid idyllic farms and woods. She discovered Marxism in university and travelled to Europe in 1979 to learn about urban guerilla groups like the Red Army Faction. An anarchist-led battle with police in Paris was "probably one of the most exciting days of my life," she recalled.

Gerry Hannah, twenty-five, grew up in the Vancouver suburbs and was semi-famous as Gerry Useless, the bass player for the popular Vancouver punk band the Subhumans.

Belmas was twenty, part of the group for two years, joining with her boyfriend, Hannah. She too had a middle-class background. Peaceful protests, she decided, weren't working.

Doug Stewart, twenty-five, was the group's technical wizard, happily poring over bomb-making manuals and exploring security weak points.

They came together in a communal one-and-a-half-storey house in Burnaby, a Vancouver suburb, in 1980. The house was a centre of anarchist and protest activity. They shoplifted or Dumpster-dived for food, organized protests, produced pamphlets and posters, and stole what they needed. Taylor, then twenty, had made the news when he hit then Conservative leader Joe Clark with a cream pie during a 1977 Vancouver visit.

The ideology was fuzzy, but the goals were clear: Disrupt the established order; challenge all institutions; and fight a long list of wrongs, from pollution to prisons to poverty.

And have fun. The fact was that being a revolutionary, risks and all, was exciting. Belmas liked buying second-hand clothes for disguises; Hansen revelled in the rush of crime.

Hansen's arrival from Toronto brought change to the group. They began to talk more about guns and false identities and robberies to fund real guerrilla acts, less about symbolic protests.

It started small. They vandalized a mining company office in downtown Vancouver in April 1981 to protest marine pollution, throwing jars of paint and rotting fish through the windows in a nighttime raid. No one paid attention.

Hannah and Belmas, then just eighteen, were involved in a second, slightly more effective, effort to vandalize the office. At least it rated a few paragraphs on an inside page of the newspaper.

Then Belmas proposed travelling to Victoria to attack the Environment Ministry that approved the mine's plans. A night attack would draw attention to the pollution on the north coast. "Plus it would be fun," Belmas added.

This time, they threw highway flares as well as paint through the windows. There was smoke and water damage and a front-page story in the *Victoria Times Colonist*. But the media called them "yahoos." For people who wanted to be revolutionaries, that stung.

They wanted to be taken seriously. If small actions don't work, there are only two choices—go bigger, or give up on guerrilla acts as a tool of change. The five weren't ready to give up.

Over the next year, they prepared. Hansen got a firearms certificate and legally bought a rifle, a Ruger Mini-14. One gun was not enough; in November, a break-in at a gun collector's home let them grab twelve handguns, semi-automatic rifles, and shotguns. They diligently practised shooting in the mountains near Squamish and stockpiled ammunition.

Real actions took money, and robbery was the guerrilla way. Their first two attempts failed. But Hansen successfully pulled a gun and grabbed a bag of money from a grocery store manager on his way to the bank. They stockpiled fake IDs and studied bomb making.

They picked targets. Litton Industries of Toronto made guidance systems for U.S. cruise missiles. The arms race, the group reasoned, threatened the world and enriched a few. BC Hydro was building a transmission line that damaged the environment and would lead to more industry on Vancouver Island. Both deserved to be attacked.

Surprisingly easily, they stole hundreds of kilograms of dynamite from highway work sites. Idealism, naiveté, arrogance, thrill-seeking, fuzzy ideology, romance, both political and personal, and groupthink drove them on.

A year after the attack on the Environment Ministry, the group was ready for another "action" on Vancouver Island.

On May 30, 1982, a sunny afternoon, Hansen and Stewart cut the fence around an almost completed transformer substation, part of the controversial transmission line. The substation was in the woods near the island's east coast; there was no security. They set up five explosive charges, detonators, and timers. At 1:30 a.m., when they were back in Vancouver drinking coffee, 160 kilograms of dynamite rocked the substation. Windows rattled kilometres away and the explosion was heard fifty kilometres away. The transformers, a crane, and other equipment were wrecked. The total damage was almost $4 million.

Direct Action claimed credit and issued a statement to the media.

But again, the response was disappointing. There was news coverage. BC Hydro offered a reward. Police launched a big investigation. But, Taylor noted days later, the public didn't really pay much attention. (That can be partly explained by the group's media statement linking the bombing to "the ecological destruction and the human oppression inherent in the industrial societies of the corporate machine in the West and the communist machine in the East" and "the sinister bonds that underlie … oppressive human relations." And partly by the fact British Columbians rejected political violence.)

They were undeterred. Plans were already under way for the Litton bombing. Hansen, Taylor, and Belmas drove to Toronto in late September, conscious of the hundreds of kilograms of dynamite riding with them. That wasn't the only reason the trip was tense. Ann Hansen and Brent Taylor were in a relationship, but she was convinced he was flirting, and maybe sleeping, with the much younger Belmas. Even revolutionaries get jealous.

They prepared, casing the Litton plant, stealing the vehicles they would need. And on October 14, they struck.

It was a disaster. The warning to Litton security wasn't understood. The dynamite exploded eleven minutes ahead of schedule, before the building was cleared. The blast and shrapnel injured three police officers, five Litton employees, and three people driving on the nearby highway.

Terry Chikowski, a thirty-four-year-old Litton employee, was trying to get staff out of the building when the bomb exploded. He found himself sprawled in the rubble, his back ripped open, ribs smashed, and organs shattered. Doctors worked seven hours to save him. Employee Barry Blunden's skull was fractured.

The three bombers were back in their apartment watching TV when the program was interrupted by a news bulletin, with horrific scenes of damage and a reporter talking to a victim with blood pouring from a head wound. Belmas started crying. Hansen contemplated suicide. Taylor talked about fleeing to the United States.

The bombing was attacked by virtually everyone involved in the protest movement against Litton and the arms race. Two communiqués issued by Taylor and the group—each about 2,000 words long—did nothing to increase support. One attempted to blame Litton staff and the police for the injuries because they didn't react quickly enough. It was seen as a pathetic attempt to avoid responsibility.

Undaunted, the group reunited in Vancouver to plan their next steps.

But by October 29, the massive police investigation had already identified Taylor as a suspect in the bombing. It wasn't difficult. Taylor had been a high-profile activist since the Joe Clark pie incident, and there were obvious links between the BC Hydro and Litton bombings.

And Canada's community of potential bombers was small. It wasn't hard to draw up a list of suspects, or surprising that Taylor was on it.

They continued planning, working with an associated cell, the Wimmin's Fire Brigade, on arson attacks on Red Hot Video stores that sold violent pornography.

But as Hansen cased the stores, the RCMP were watching. The attacks went ahead—two stores were set on fire with gasoline bombs. Belmas failed in her attack on a third store when the Molotov cocktail wouldn't ignite.

She was luckier than Hansen. Her attempt to use gasoline to burn one of the stores worked, but a fireball engulfed her. "I vaguely remember my coat being on fire and the smell of singed hair," she recalled. Her trip to the emergency room, hours after a high-profile arson attack, was hardly likely to go unnoticed.

Wiretaps, listening devices, surveillance, secret searches. The net was tightening. The group's plans for robbing a Brink's truck and bombing an air base and new Coast Guard icebreakers were being monitored by police. The listening devices captured discussions of the past bombings that would be persuasive in court.

And then the RCMP moved. The five—Hansen, Taylor, Stewart, Belmas, Hannah—left at dawn for Squamish, for their last gun practice before the Brink's robbery. On a narrow, twisting part of the highway, traffic was stopped for construction, with a flagman letting cars through a few at a time. Their truck crept forward, until it was the lone vehicle left.

But the construction workers were in fact heavily armed RCMP emergency response team officers. In barely a minute, the five were in handcuffs.

Direct Action was done.

Ultimately, Belmas was sentenced to fifteen years in prison, Taylor to twenty-two years, and Hansen to life. Stewart was sentenced to six years and Hannah to ten years.

All are now free. None has fully renounced his or her actions.

BOMB ON A TRAIN

The Kettle Valley train was on its daily run west through the mountains from Nelson, on the leg from Brilliant to Grand Forks. It was only about 100 kilometres, but the steam engine hauled the train at less than thirty kilometres per hour—much less on the steep uphill grades.

It was just before 1:00 a.m. on October 29, 1924. Passengers were dozing, or sleeping, the pine forests rolling by in the dark, a skiff of snow on the ground.

"Lordly"—Peter Verigin, the powerful, charismatic head of a large Doukhobor community—was sitting halfway down Car 1586, a first-class coach, on the right side. Beside him, at the window, sat seventeen-year-old Mary Strelaeff, his constant travelling companion.

Two seats in front, newly elected Conservative MLA John McKie was heading to Victoria for his first legislative session.

Another nineteen people were scattered around the car, taking occasional breaks in the small enclosed smoking cabin at the rear.

Some of them stirred as the train stopped for eighteen minutes at the Farron Summit. It took on water and added a café car to the six-car train before starting the downhill run toward Grand Forks. It was a dark night, the moon a sliver.

Four minutes after leaving Fallon, Car 1586 exploded. Bodies and debris flew into the night, and a fireball swept through the car. Brakes shrieked as the train shuddered to a halt.

Conductor Joseph Turner had just passed through the coach and into the baggage car. The blast blew its door off, sending it hurtling almost the length of the car and showering him with broken glass.

Verigin, McKie, and two others died instantly. Four people were grievously injured and loaded into the sleeper car and rushed to Castlegar, a jolting, nightmarish trip. Two died en route; the other two once they arrived. Another eleven people were treated for injuries.

The blast was tremendous. Cst. G. F. Killam of the British Columbia Provincial Police was the first officer on the scene the next morning. The coach was still smouldering, "with nothing but charred embers and ironwork remaining."

One body burned almost beyond recognition rested against a rear wheel of the car.

Hakim Singh, who had been sitting at the rear of the car, was found without his head, a chunk of his chest, and his right arm. His missing arm was found almost eleven metres away.

Verigin was face down, "with a considerable number of wounds ... but easily recognizable." His body had been tossed about eight metres by the blast. McKie's corpse was thrown seven or eight metres beyond Verigin.

Pieces of the coach had been blasted ten metres up the mountainside, and clothes and baggage were strewn all around the area.

Police and Canadian Pacific Railway investigators concluded almost immediately that a bomb had caused the explosion. As they picked through the wreckage, they found bits of a clock and dry cell batteries—a possible detonator.

But who planted the powerful bomb? Peter Verigin was the obvious target, but he had a long list of enemies, inside and outside the Doukhobor community.

To many Doukhobors, Verigin was saintly. He wielded immense personal power. He was six feet tall, good-looking, with a better education than most of the community. With his slicked-back dark hair and full black moustache, he was an imposing figure who accepted his right to rule over the faithful.

But not everyone agreed. A small but fierce Doukhobor faction dubbed the Freedomites thought Verigin was embracing modern ways—like mechanized farming—and becoming too materialistic. At public protests, they stripped naked to show their disdain for possessions, a gesture not well received in small communities.

More dangerously, the Freedomites had burned schools and the homes and barns of neighbours who they thought had strayed from the faith. Just six months earlier, Verigin's summer house and office at Brilliant, just across the Columbia River from Castlegar, had been torched.

Doukhobor communities were also having increasing conflicts with governments and their neighbours.

About 7,500 Doukhobors had been welcomed into Canada in 1899, part of Interior Minister Clifford Sifton's plan to populate the West.

The Doukhobors needed somewhere to go. Their commitment to communal living and pacifism and their rejection of the authority of established churches and the state infuriated the Russian government. Their refusal to serve in the military was a particular irritant, and they faced increasing persecution. Advocates like writer Leo Tolstoy championed their cause.

When Verigin suggested emigration as a solution, the Russian authorities were quick to agree.

But the initial Canadian welcome had grown chilly. The First World War had brought suspicion of anyone not of British origin. The Doukhobors' refusal to fight made them a particular target. Businesses in neighbouring communities feared competition from rapidly expanding Doukhobor enterprises. And there was simple prejudice.

Governments were also becoming troubled by the independence of the Doukhobors—their refusal to swear allegiance to the Crown or to send their children to public schools (or often, to any schools). Public education was a tool of assimilation, and the Doukhobor boycott undermined the government's agenda.

Theories about the explosion abounded. Verigin had initially supported the revolutionary government in Russia, and even discussed the Doukhobors' return. But he became increasingly critical of Vladimir Lenin. Some in the Doukhobor community saw a Russian plot behind the bomb.

Others suspected Verigin's son, Peter P. Verigin, of masterminding the blast to clear the way for his own ascension to power. He did eventually succeed his father.

And still others remain convinced the blast was simply an accident. Rail safety standards were low, and people in rural communities thought nothing of boarding a train with the explosives bought to clear their land or explore a claim.

The bomber—and it was almost certainly a bomb—was never identified. But the loss of Verigin dealt a major blow to the Doukhobors. The community was weakened by leadership disputes, and government pressure intensified. The Freedomites attracted more supporters, and became enmeshed in decades-long conflicts with government and neighbouring communities.

And the deaths of Peter Verigin and seven other people on that October night remain unsolved.

ESCAPE TO THE WILD

Simon Gunanoot walked into the vast wilderness near Hazelton on June 19, 1906, as an accused "murdering Indian."

He walked out thirteen years later a folk hero.

Gunanoot was Gitksan, handsome and successful, a skilled and respected trapper and rancher and businessman. He had a lot to leave behind.

But a long drunken night in a sleazy frontier bar had ended with two men shot dead. White men. Gunanoot knew he would be the prime suspect.

So he headed home and told his wife and family to gather what they could and be ready to flee into the woods. The family would hide out for more than a decade, eluding a series of massive, costly manhunts.

Gunanoot was born in Kispiox, a Native village about thirteen kilometres up the Skeena River from Hazelton. He had grown up learning to live in the woods, trapping, hunting, fishing.

But Gunanoot—or Simon Johnson, as he was christened—had also gone to a mission school and could read and write, though not well.

He was a big, handsome guy of thirty-one in 1906, with thick dark hair, a generous mouth, and a frankly appraising and open gaze. And, by all accounts, he was hard-working and smart. Gunanoot trapped in the winter, but instead of selling his furs to local intermediaries, he travelled to Victoria or

Seattle to get a better price. Then he would buy goods there to sell in his store in Kispiox, again cutting out the middlemen.

Hazelton wasn't much to look at. Main Street was a wide wagon track with wooden boardwalks, frozen in the winter and a muddy mire when it rained. There were a handful of wood-plank businesses with soaring false fronts and big hopes.

But the outpost had a run of good fortune. It was the prime launching place for prospectors trying to cash in on the 1869 Omineca gold rush.

And in 1891, the first sternwheeler fought its way up the Skeena from the Pacific, and freight service was launched. Hazelton was as far as the boats could go, and they pulled up on the riverbank to unload just metres away from drying fishing nets. Packers were needed to take the goods on to their destinations. Gunanoot used a fine riverside ranch as the base for his pack operation.

On June 18, 1906, a warm Monday, Gunanoot's nineteen-year-old wife, Sarah, sent him to another village to buy some fish.

Gunanoot decided to stop for a drink and pulled his stallion up at the Two Mile Hotel. Two Mile—named for its distance from Hazelton—was notorious for its bar and red-light district. The hotel was disreputable, a place for drunkenness, gambling, and prostitution, according to the local police.

The smoky, dark interior was inviting. Gunanoot stayed until dawn, drinking with a rough crowd that included Alex MacIntosh, a short, powerful packer with a rival outfit who had just finished time in jail for bootlegging.

Then things went bad, as they will in bars. It's not clear what started the fight. Some say MacIntosh insulted Gunanoot's young wife, or said she had sex with his friend Max Leclair. Others blame Gunanoot. What's not disputed is that he and MacIntosh fought, and that MacIntosh slashed Gunanoot's cheek open with a knife and bloodied his nose. MacIntosh cut his own finger.

MacIntosh's employer halted the brawl and made the men shake hands. But witnesses said they heard Gunanoot threaten revenge as he left the saloon.

The next morning, MacIntosh's body was found sprawled beside the trail from the Two Mile, a bullet hole in his back. He had been shot off his horse. A few hours later, Leclair's body was found.

Gunanoot was the obvious suspect. But by the time police showed up at his house in Kispiox, he was gone. Sarah, their three children, his parents, his brother-in-law Peter Himadam—also a suspect—and his wife had all vanished.

The hunt started small, with special constables sworn in to support the local officer. They had no success, at least in part because Gunanoot—a superb shot, hunter, and woodsman—was a formidable presence. It was easy for police to imagine danger or death behind every pine tree or rocky outcrop.

More and more police and special constables were thrown into the hunt through that summer and fall, to no avail. Police, bounty hunters—eventually even detectives from the famed Pinkerton's agency brought in from the United States—all tried and failed to find Gunanoot and his band. The provincial government posted a $1,000 reward, huge money in 1906. The lack of success was a galling failure for police and the government.

And a worrying one. First Nations in the northwest were locked in disputes with the government about incursions into their lands, including newly constructed canneries that brought pressure on fish stocks, and a need for larger reserves.

Gunanoot's successful flight made the government look dangerously weak, the *Kamloops Standard* warned. "Because of the non-capture of the murderers Simon Gunanoot and Peter Himadam, the Indians in this district are becoming very cheeky and defying the law."

The *British Colonist* newspaper insisted this "Indian murderer, who is skulking in the wilds of northern British Columbia," was undermining the principles of British justice.

But the province was hardly Britain. About 290,000 people were spread over 945,000 square kilometres. (Great Britain had 135 times as many people in a little more than one-third the area.) Just getting to Hazelton from Victoria took five days by sternwheeler, much longer in the winter. The mountains and river valleys were wild and unmapped.

Frustrated searchers reported another problem. They had counted on information from people who lived in the area and had seen Gunanoot and his group, especially as the reward climbed.

Instead, they ran into a wall of silence—not just from Natives, but from settlers and the white community. Gunanoot was respected by both groups, and settlers didn't want trouble with their Native neighbours.

"Everyone in the North sympathizes with Gunanoot," the *Toronto Star*'s correspondent reported. "People of Hazelton declare that a white man would have killed the two ruffians who debauched his wife long before Simon did the job." (The claim that Gunanoot's wife had been assaulted was widely accepted on little or no evidence.)

Even the Methodist minister in Kispiox decided not to report a visit by Gunanoot to settle some business affairs.

It was an amazing feat. In the time that Gunanoot was eluding justice, the province's population more than doubled, more than 60,000 Canadians died in the First World War, and the first cars came to Hazelton. The Skeena paddle-wheelers gave up the difficult run, replaced in 1912 by a rail line that brought passengers and freight from Prince Rupert and sparked another boom in the region. Emily Carr visited Kispiox to sketch and paint the totems.

Almost everything in the outside world changed, but Gunanoot and his family survived and prospered, continuing to trap and trade and amassing a fortune estimated at $75,000 by some sources.

But it was a hard life. By 1919, Gunanoot was forty-four. Two more children had been born in the thirteen years in the wilderness, and he wanted all five children to be educated. And the bitterly cold winters were becoming harder to take.

It was time to give up. Gunanoot made careful plans for his surrender. Through intermediaries, he contacted Stuart Henderson, a former MLA and a skilled lawyer trusted by Native communities. The Scottish-born Henderson dressed more like a small-town rancher than the high-powered lawyer that he was, but had defended twenty-eight murder cases. His fee—rumoured at $20,000—was enormous, but worth every penny to Gunanoot if it kept him from hanging or serving a life sentence in a small jail cell. (For him, it was hard to decide which would be a worse fate.)

On June 25, 1919, Henderson arrived in Hazelton around noon. George Beirnes, a rancher, packer, and friend of Gunanoot, went into the woods and came back with the fugitive. Together, the three men strode into the Hazelton police station and jail, a storey-and-a-half wood-sided building with a steep roof to shed the winter snow and piles of firewood along one side.

Gunanoot surrendered to a surprised and puzzled constable.

He emerged from the bush a folk hero, "of magnificent physique, one of the finest specimens of the real Indian," the *British Colonist* enthused. Gunanoot was a legend—"Many stories are told by his fellow Indians of his prowess, of his ability to fell an ox with a blow of his fist, of his ability as a hunter and trapper and his fidelity to his friends."

There was celebrating in Native and non-Native communities. The continuing tensions between First Nations and settlers and miners had kept the region on edge and discouraged development. Gunanoot, as an outlaw, was seen as a potential leader of dissatisfied Natives.

This was a chance to bring about better understanding between Natives and whites, said the *Colonist*: "Much development will take place in the northern country when some troubles are thrashed out." Tourists, settlers, prospectors would all start coming to the region once they learned that the outlaws were no longer roaming the woods and that relations between Natives and whites were improved.

Gunanoot was a celebrity. He posed for a picture with the three members of the Hazelton police before being sent to New Westminster for trial, all of the men in suits and ties and waistcoats. He looked much like the leader of the group.

Henderson earned his money. He arranged a speedy trial, and easily poked holes in the evidence, helped by the long passage of time and the fact that so many of the witnesses were drunk while events unfolded. On October 8, it took a New

Westminster jury less than fifteen minutes to decide on a not-guilty verdict.

Gunanoot lived another fourteen years a free man.

TERROR IN THE SKY

On a June morning in 1985, CSIS anti-terror officers followed two Sikh men travelling from Burnaby to Vancouver Island.

One was Talwinder Singh Parmar, the forty-year-old leader of Babbar Khalsa, a terrorist organization dedicated to creating an autonomous Sikh homeland in the Punjab, avenging attacks on Sikhs in India, and enforcing its conservative version of Sikhism. The agents didn't know the identity of the other man. They called him Mr. X.

The two drove south from Nanaimo to the Duncan home of Inderjit Singh Reyat, an electrician and auto mechanic who shared their views. He was devout, a temple drummer, and his fiercely conservative religious views and strident efforts to impose his will had made him well-known at the Duncan temple. A month earlier, Parmar had asked Reyat to build a bomb. The Duncan man had found dynamite, bought clocks and batteries and electronic gear.

The next morning, the CSIS agents followed the three men as they drove a few minutes from Duncan and headed into the woods. The agents heard a loud bang.

But they didn't alert the RCMP, or ask officers to stop the men's car. They didn't do a thorough search to look for evidence of explosives.

Seventeen days later, Reyat drove onto a BC Ferry and headed for Vancouver and Parmar's neighbourhood. He stopped to buy two 12-volt batteries. On that same day, two men who have never been identified checked bags onto flights connecting with Air India flights in Japan and Toronto.

* * *

The first bomb ripped through Japan's Narita Airport as baggage was being transferred from the Vancouver flight to an Air India flight to Thailand. Two baggage handlers were killed.

Much worse was ahead. When the first bomb exploded, Air India Flight 182 was already in the air, on its way from Toronto to Delhi via London. It was early morning aboard the 747, and most of the 307 passengers were dozing. The majority were Canadians, including many heading back to visit family in India. It was a quiet time for the twenty-two crew.

Less than an hour after the Narita blast, a suitcase bomb exploded in the rear cargo hold of Flight 182. The plane split in two, lengthwise. Wreckage and passengers fell more than nine kilometres into the North Atlantic, about 190 kilometres off the coast of Ireland. There were no survivors.

And for the victims, there would be no justice.

Terrorism and mass murder had come to Canada. The country was hopelessly unprepared, despite at least a decade of warnings that a small group of militants among Canada's 140,000 Sikhs was becoming more influential, and more violent. Those warnings had included pleas for action from moderate Sikhs who feared, with good reason, the extremists among them. Ujjal Dosanjh, who would go on to become British Columbia's first Indo-Canadian premier and then an MP, had been attacked four months before the bombings and beaten brutally with an iron bar for speaking out against the militants.

Reyat settled back into his life in Duncan, heading to work at Auto-Marine Electric each day and sharing a routine with his wife, son, and three daughters. It was a pleasant town, close to the Strait of Georgia, with a Sikh community of about 2,000.

But he, Parmar, and a group of Babbar Khalsa supporters were emerging as prime suspects. The RCMP were under tremendous pressure to produce results after the terror attacks, and getting little help from CSIS, which had erased more than one-third of the tapes of wiretap evidence from Parmar's phone.

Evidence linking Reyat to the Narita bomb was building. Fragments showed the bomb was built from components that could only have come from his preparations in Duncan.

Five months after the blast, the RCMP arrested Reyat on his way home from work. They arrested Parmar and searched several other Lower Mainland locations at the same time.

The RCMP said Reyat was suspected of serious offences linked to the bombings. Parmar was just charged with possessing explosives.

If the charges were an attempt to force Reyat to provide information, they failed. Reyat's long interrogation by the RCMP produced contradictory, vague, and useless answers.

First he denied ever meeting Parmar or having anything to do with bombs. When he was told CSIS agents had witnessed the test bombing, Reyat said Parmar had asked him about making a big bomb, and he assumed it was wanted for some action in India—blowing up a bridge or something. None of the devices worked, he told two RCMP officers. Informed that Japanese investigators confirmed the bomb was housed in a Sanyo stereo tuner identical to the one he had bought at the Duncan Woolworth store, Reyat said he had given the tuner away as a gift to a virtual stranger.

Whether he was loyal, or afraid, Reyat wasn't going to tell what he knew. He offered nothing useful to police.

Parmar appeared in court dressed in the flowing robes and tall orange turban of a 400-year-old Sikh warrior group. Supporters cheered and chanted when the charge against him was dismissed.

Reyat ended up pleading guilty to minor charges of possessing a handgun and one stick of dynamite and was fined $2,000. It didn't help that CSIS used a national security provision to prevent even innocuous defence questioning of its agents.

* * *

The Indian-born Reyat had grown up in England. He knew police pressure would be unrelenting, and the family moved back to Coventry, where he took up his old job at a Jaguar car factory, settled into a modest house, and attended a local temple.

In Canada, the Air India investigation was running into more brick walls. But the evidence linking Reyat to the Narita bombing was becoming stronger.

In February 1988, British police working with Canadian prosecutors swooped in on Reyat as he drove to work. The extradition battle lasted for almost a year due to high-priced British lawyers enlisted in Reyat's defence. But the British courts eventually ordered his return to Canada to face trial on manslaughter and explosives charges linked to the Narita bombing.

After a sixty-two-day trial, he was found guilty in May 1991. The court found Reyat had aided the actual murderers by building the bomb, although he might not have known how it would be used. Reyat didn't testify.

His lawyer read supporting statements at the sentencing hearing, including letters from Reyat's three oldest children. "It's been 3 1/2 years since I haven't seen him at home. I love him very much," ten-year-old Pritpal wrote. "I really, really need my daddy now."

Reyat was sentenced to ten years in prison.

* * *

The investigation lagged. Every June 23, families mourned, and wondered how such a terrible crime could be committed with impunity.

Finally, in the fall of 2000, fourteen years after the bombings, prosecutors laid 331 murder charges against two men they say helped plan the terror attack. Ripudaman Singh Malik was a multi-millionaire Vancouver businessman and militant; Ajaib Singh Bagri was a Kamloops sawmill worker who had made speeches calling for Sikhs to kill 50,000 Hindu "dogs" to avenge attacks on Sikhs in India. (Talwinder Parmar was already dead, apparently captured and killed by Indian police in 1992 after he returned to the country.)

Seven months later, they laid similar charges against Reyat, still in jail for the Narita deaths.

Reyat was the key. And in a controversial decision, the Crown agreed to let him plead guilty to manslaughter charges in the Air India bombing, and agreed to a plea bargain that would see him serve just five more years.

He was remorseful, he told the court. In return for the light sentence, he promised to testify truthfully in the trial of Malik and Bagri. A deal with the devil, some said.

When the time came to fulfil the bargain and tell the truth in court during the trial of Malik and Bagri, Reyat simply refused. He lied, dodged questions, claimed not to remember events that had cost him years behind bars. He kept dynamite around in case he might want to dislodge a stump someday, he said. He let "Mr. X," the man who came to watch the bomb test, stay in his house, with his family, for several days but never knew his first or last names.

It was transparently corrupt. The trial judge called him an "unmitigated liar."

"His evidence was patently and pathetically fabricated in an attempt to minimize his involvement in his crime to an extreme degree, while refusing to reveal relevant information he clearly possesses," the judge said. "His hollow expression of remorse was a bitter pill for the families of the victims. If he harboured even the slightest degree of genuine remorse, he would have been more forthcoming."

But without evidence from Reyat, Malik and Bagri were acquitted. The fifteen-year investigation had cost some $130 million.

Reyat was charged with perjury as a result of his bizarre testimony and sentenced to nine years. And the worst mass murderers in Canada's history went unpunished.

GANGLAND EDEN

Police Chief Walter Mulligan looked like the man to clean up Vancouver's sinful ways when he stepped up to the department's top job on January 24, 1947.

Six foot two and 220 pounds. Handsome and always sharply dressed, in uniform or a suit. Streetwise, after a stint keeping the peace on Broadway between Granville and Main.

And, based on his rapid twenty-year rise through the ranks to become the Vancouver department's youngest chief at forty-two, smart and politically savvy, with all the right connections.

The Liverpool-born Mulligan faced a tough task. Vancouver was a wide open town.

The laws, especially around vices, reflected the 1930s views of conservative politicians from small towns and rural communities.

But the war had changed everything. Vancouver was booming, and young men and women just out of the service wanted to have some fun. They were through being ordered around. They had fought for their country—and gambled and drank. They weren't going to be told what to do once they were home and had some money to spend.

It was time for fun. For nightclubs. Parties. But in Vancouver, grim beer halls were the only legal places to buy drinks. They could only serve beer, and only one brand. They had to be attached to a hotel and couldn't sell food or non-alcoholic drinks, and women were barred from the large men-only sections. No drinking in restaurants or nightclubs, unless they were members-only "private clubs," where patrons were supposed to bring their own bottles.

But people wanted a drink with their dinner or while they danced. The dry laws were ignored or ridiculed.

Any time the law and social values are wildly out of sync, there is money to be made. Speakeasies and bootleggers flourished, and illegal profits soared.

That meant corruption. Police couldn't stop the booze trade—it was too big. And they couldn't ignore it. So they had to make some arrests. A bribe could encourage police to shut down a rival, and not your blind pig.

It wasn't just alcohol. Gambling, prostitution and, increasingly, drugs were all booming in the postwar years. So was police corruption.

Mulligan came in as a reformer. He complained publicly that officers on the vice squad had let gambling dens operate. "These places could not operate without police knowledge and sanction," he told city council. That didn't win him friends on the force.

He had played rough and stepped on a lot of toes on his way to the top job. Once he got it, he made unpopular changes—putting detectives back into uniform and limiting stints on the detective and vice squads to two years to prevent cops and crooks becoming too cozy.

And Mulligan promoted his own people into top jobs, and pushed out others. He angered the powerful police union—a formidable enemy—by ignoring seniority.

Which all might have been okay. If he had got results.

But Vancouver was still a wide open city under Mulligan, legendary British Columbia broadcaster Jack Webster recalled. "Gambling, prostitution and bootlegging were rampant."

"The police force was something else again—rotten at the top."

Reporters talked about police corruption, but they didn't write about it.

Still, Mulligan's rule was unthreatened. He cut a fine figure riding a horse in the annual PNE parade, or dressed in a tam and Highland garb for a Scottish festival.

But trouble was brewing. Mulligan's powerful ally and champion, Mayor Gerry McGeer, died of a heart attack. Opposition on the police force—especially from the union leadership—was growing. The corruption whispers, some from inside the force, grew louder.

And despite steady increases in the number of officers, crime was getting worse. Gangs were getting more violent, and dumping bodies carelessly.

Heroin had hit the city, with Mulligan saying Vancouver had more than 1,500 addicts by the end of 1954. They stole to get money for drugs. In one six-week stretch in late 1954, there were seventy-four armed robberies in the city—banks, corner stores, anywhere with money. Mulligan even talked about a machine-gun equipped flying squad to battle the robbers. (Mulligan also proposed dealing with the heroin problem by sending the addicts to an isolated island or, alternately, supplying them with drugs.)

Still, Mulligan might have been fine, if not for Ray Munro.

Munro was a thirty-two-year-old reporter who wanted to be a star. Handsome, dashing, a pilot and adventurer, Munro put himself at the centre of every story, the crusading hero who would risk all to reveal the truth. He even talked another reporter into going out with him, the two dressed as women, to try and catch a rapist in Stanley Park. (They succeeded.)

Munro had stints at the *Sun* and the *Province*, leaving the latter when the paper wouldn't run his stories of police corruption.

So he hooked up with Lou Ruby, the Toronto publisher of *Flash Weekly*, a scandal sheet. Munro would head a new *Flash* west coast bureau, and the paper would publish a Vancouver edition.

On June 15, 1955, the first issue hit the streets with a screaming headline launching a full attack on Mulligan and police corruption:

"RAPE OF VANCOUVER! MUNRO TEARS MASK FROM CROOKED LAW IN GANGLAND EDEN."

The lead was just as dramatic. "A police chief who took a piggy bank—a deputy chief whose secret activities and fits of rage are the talk of a neighbourhood—crooked detectives and enough intrigue to make the fictitious Mike Hammer look like a Lavender Lad—that's the talk of this port city today!"

The prose was over the top, and the tease about revelations still to come—"How the Syndicate Captured City Hall" and "Society Playboy's Sinister Double Life"—was sensational.

Munro had good sources. The claim that Mulligan stole a piggy bank came from an ex-cop, who said the two of them were investigating a break-in when Mulligan grabbed a glass piggy bank. They each got eleven dollars, he recalled.

Mulligan knew he was in trouble. The police commission and politicians were treating the allegations seriously. He took the offensive on June 23, suing Munro and *Flash*.

The next day, everything fell apart. *Flash* had reported that Detective Sergeant Len Cuthbert, a thirty-year veteran of the VPD, collected bribes from gamblers and shared them with Mulligan—and that he "snitched" on fellow officers about corruption.

Cuthbert, a fifty-four-year-old father of three—including an eighteen-month-old son—was devastated. On June 24, a bright spring day, he reported early to the grim brick police headquarters on Main Street. Supt. Harry Whelan interviewed him about corruption, finishing a little after 8:00 a.m.

Cuthbert made his way to the detective room and asked other officers to tell his wife he had sold his boat and paid their property tax.

Then he went into an interview room, pulled out his .38-calibre service revolver, and shot himself in the chest.

Two detectives rushed into the room, where Cuthbert was muttering, "I'm sorry I missed my heart." He had missed; his life was saved.

The suicide attempt made the scandal too big to ignore. The police board suspended Mulligan within hours, and the provincial government announced a royal commission into police corruption.

The inquiry, headed by lawyer R. H. Tupper, was a sensation. There was testimony of graft and bribes, and a parade of officers who seemed unable to remember anything on the witness stand. Reputations were smeared daily.

Cuthbert, still recovering, testified that as head of the gambling squad he had split bribes with Mulligan, and shared them with other detectives in on the scam.

Whelan, the superintendent who questioned Cuthbert before his suicide attempt, had already testified about that interview. He was scheduled to appear again, and warned that Mulligan's fierce lawyer, Tom Norris, would raise the suicides of his father and daughter.

He, too, chose to shoot himself in the chest, in his home. Unlike Cuthbert, he succeeded, dying on the way to hospital on August 5.

In September, the "Mystery Lady" took the witness stand. She testified under her maiden name, Helen Douglas, and wore an obvious, dramatic disguise—floppy blue hat, blonde wig, heavy makeup. She had been Mulligan's mistress for several years, she said. He had given her jewelry and money to help buy a house, and taken her with him to a police chiefs' gathering in Montreal. Asked how Mulligan could pay for all this, she said, "I had the impression it didn't come from his salary." (Douglas faced a savage examination by Mulligan's lawyer, who sought to portray her as a vengeful, promiscuous liar.)

Mulligan saw the writing on the wall. His original lawyer, Tom Norris, had quit the case after what he described as an attempt at blackmail by Munro, still chasing scoops for *Flash*.

He was replaced by Jay Gould, who was appalled by the inquiry's willingness to accept hearsay evidence. Witnesses repeated what someone else had told them, but Gould could not question the original source of the allegations.

On October 12, Gould denounced the process as an "inquisition" that wrongly smeared his client. They would no longer participate, he said. Mulligan would answer any charges in court, he said, where the process was fair.

Mulligan then went to the police commission. Fire me, he said. I can longer do the job. The commission obliged, and he simply pulled up stakes and left the country. He headed to Los

Angeles, and landed a job as an airport limousine dispatcher.

The inquiry continued, but the drama was over. Tupper's final report found Mulligan and Cuthbert had committed criminal offences, but that he had been unable to identify anyone else involved. The police commission and politicians shared the blame for shoddy oversight.

No one was charged. No one was fired. "A whitewash," Webster tersely summarized the entire process.

The city hired George Archer, a thirty-five-year veteran of the RCMP, to replace Mulligan. He was a strict disciplinarian, and credited with bringing order to the force.

After eight years in California, Mulligan retired to Oak Bay, a quiet municipality that's part of Greater Victoria, living in part on his Vancouver police pension.

Mulligan had grown prize-winning flowers while chief. Oak Bay was a perfect place for his hobby. He died March 27, 1987.

THE FALLEN BISHOP

Long before seventy-one-year-old Bishop Hubert O'Connor showed up on a June day in 1998 for a healing circle, the Esk'etemc people of Alkali Lake knew all about pain and redemption.

The reserve, home to about 400 people, is in a beautiful but harsh near-desert east of the Fraser River and south of Williams Lake. For decades, the reserve had been defined by deprivation, drinking, violence, and poverty. "Alcohol Lake," people had called it, until an extraordinary effort by community leaders brought transformation and hope in the 1970s.

For the people of Alkali Lake, the abandoned St. Joseph's Indian Residential School was a symbol of suffering. For ninety years, children had been taken away to the school outside Williams Lake. Too many came back broken.

O'Connor ran the school for years in the 1960s. In 1996, he was convicted of raping a young Native woman during his time at the school and then freed on appeal. O'Connor had become the face of a system that took children from their families, punished them for speaking their language, and subjected them to privation and abuse.

And his case had come to symbolize the failure of the Canadian justice system in dealing with crimes against First Nations people.

O'Connor, born in Quebec on February 17, 1928, didn't become a Roman Catholic priest until he was twenty-seven. He joined a missionary order and was sent west in 1961 to become principal of St. Joseph's Indian Residential School in Williams Lake.

It was a powerful position in a formidable institution. The school was already seventy-five years old, part of a network of eighty residential schools across Canada. The Indian Affairs Department made attendance mandatory for children, who were taken from their families by force if necessary. They were allowed to go home for one month a year, and were cut off from family and community.

The goal was to solve "the Indian problem" by stripping the children of all traces of their culture. As Prime Minister Stephen Harper said in a 2008 apology, "to kill the Indian in the child."

There were, defenders point out, caring teachers and students who thrived. But the overall legacy was darker. O'Connor and those running the schools had near-absolute authority over powerless children and families. More than 4,000 children died across Canada. Government researchers used malnourished children as guinea pigs in nutrition studies. Sexual and physical abuse were rampant.

And thousands of children grew up disconnected from family and community, without the knowledge or experience to parent their own children. For survivors of abuse, the trauma devastated their lives. Guilt and shame led to silence.

O'Connor ran St. Joseph's for seven years, a position of great power and little accountability. The church leadership regarded him so highly that in 1971 he was appointed bishop of Whitehorse, then bishop of Prince George in 1986.

But across Canada, residential school survivors were beginning to move beyond shame to tell their stories of abuse.

A tall, soft-spoken RCMP constable, Bob Grinstead, started hearing about cases of sexual and physical abuse at St. Joseph's. He was originally from Toronto, and didn't even know residential schools existed until he joined the force. The investigation was painful for him and the victims. Many had become abusers themselves, or fallen into addictions or killed themselves. "It struck me that an awful lot of the people I was looking for weren't around anymore."

When he dropped in to visit Marilyn Belleau in Alkali Lake, she broke two decades' of silence. O'Connor had raped her, she said.

Belleau was still hesitant to talk about it. She had a daughter. The memories were dark and painful. But once she had told Grinstead, she sought counselling and shared more of the past.

She was nineteen, a devout, shy former student who worked at the school as a seamstress and helped with its bagpipe band, which travelled and gave concerts. O'Connor had taken her alone to a drive-in movie and tried to grab her and kiss her. When O'Connor asked her to his room a few days later, she thought he wanted to apologize.

Instead, he had turned down his bed and placed a towel in the middle of the sheet. He told her to take off her clothes and lie down.

Belleau froze for what seemed an eternity. "I was so scared. I felt like I didn't have any choice. He was my boss and he was a priest."

"I had never ever let a man see my body, naked. I felt I didn't have any choice but to do as he said. So I took all my clothes off. I was feeling ashamed and shy."

O'Connor raped her. She lay there, separated her mind from her body, and pretended she was somewhere else. "Like at home walking around in the tall grass, in our meadow. With the wind blowing in my face."

The rapes would be repeated more than ten times over the next few years. When she became pregnant, O'Connor gave her a choice: He could send her to an institution for unwed mothers, or arrange a stay in a private home in Vancouver. No one could know. He registered as the father after the birth, but didn't use his real first name and made up an occupation.

Belleau named her daughter Maria Ann and held her close in the hospital, until she was taken away. Two decades later, Belleau would be devastated once again when she learned the daughter she had never seen grow up had died in a car crash at twenty-three.

Soon, five more victims came forward with similar stories. They had been students or staff, young Native women and girls, and O'Connor, the priest and leader, had sexually abused them.

They were difficult cases. The crimes were decades old. Speaking out meant reliving painful stories and challenging powerful institutions, and trusting a justice system that had rarely worked for Native people.

But on Monday, February 4, 1991, the word spread through Alkali Lake and other First Nations communities. Thirty years after he took over the school, O'Connor had been charged with six sex-related assaults. Another Oblate priest who had worked at the school had already pleaded guilty to sexually assaulting seventeen boys at the school and in other communities over twenty-five years, and a third Oblate brother faced additional charges of sexually assaulting boys at the school.

The women were fearful about testifying and reliving those days and about the cumbersome judicial process.

They were right to be fearful. The justice system did not work.

The women testified at a preliminary hearing in 1992, and O'Connor was ordered to stand trial on four charges—two of rape and two of indecent assault.

The trial began in June. But the Crown prosecutor had ignored the judge's instructions and failed to disclose evidence to O'Connor's lawyer, mainly notes from the victims' counselling sessions. The judge stayed the charges and ended the trial.

Two years later, the British Columbia Court of Appeal ordered a new trial. But O'Connor, with seemingly unlimited money for legal fees, appealed that decision to the Supreme Court of Canada. He lost, but four years had gone by before the new trial began in June 1996.

O'Connor was found guilty on charges of rape and indecent assault, and sentenced to two-and-a-half years in prison.

But less than seven months later, he was free. His lawyers had appealed again, and in March 1998 the court had overturned the indecent assault conviction and ordered yet another trial on the rape charge.

Almost six years had been spent in court. The case would now rest on Belleau's testimony alone, against O'Connor's claim that the sex was consensual. And she wasn't sure she could summon the strength to go through the ordeal again.

O'Connor's lawyer proposed an alternative. A healing circle, a traditional Native ceremony, where O'Connor would face the victims and the community and accept accountability. It was a difficult, controversial decision. To many, it seemed a poor substitute for criminal proceedings in a case of rape.

But Belleau agreed. On Monday, June 18, 1998, O'Connor and government officials drove along Dog Creek Road to Alkali Lake. The circle opened with a solemn ceremony, led by an Elder, and the first segment brought a small group together. Belleau confronted O'Connor, describing her pain and the damage that he had done. O'Connor, now seventy, apologized, though he never acknowledged that he raped her.

Almost forty people took part, including family members, Elders, and others who were directly involved. They talked about their pain, not just resulting from O'Connor's acts, but from the residential school experience overall.

By the final phase, the long, narrow community hall was crowded with seventy people. O'Connor and the region's bishop read formal apologies. O'Connor's effort was oddly stilted. He talked about "the complainants," and his "very difficult time" over the last eight years. But he did apologize for breaching his vow of celibacy and "unacceptable behaviour" and the harm he had done.

For Marilyn Belleau, it was enough. The circle ended with prayers, songs, drumming, and dancing. A long, terrible journey was over. "I came out of it feeling really much lighter," she said, not just due to the healing circle but the whole process of coming forward. "That cloak of shame, I've let go of that."

SAVING THE CHILDREN

William Lepine was on a mission to save the children. Only he understood the danger. Only he could rescue them from a nuclear holocaust. Even if it meant a killing spree.

Lepine didn't know why he was chosen. He was twenty-seven, just a guy who had left the United States and worked in the orchards around Summerside for a few years. It was easy to fit in there in 1970, even if you were a bit different. The Okanagan Valley was a stop on the hippie pilgrimage to Vancouver. There was work picking fruit, and there were farmers who would let you pitch tents in their orchards if you helped bring in the peaches or cherries.

But orchard work was seasonal. Lepine found something more stable in Creston, a quiet town in the south Kootenay, about ten kilometres from the Idaho border. He settled in as a gardener and maintenance worker with the municipality in 1971.

It was a good place to live. About 3,000 people, with the Purcell Mountains rising above the Kootenay River valley. Though Creston had its demons too. A year before Lepine arrived, a logger named Dale Nelson went on a drunken, deadly rampage, killing eight people, including five young children.

Once Lepine had made Creston home, a more interesting job came along. The Dr. Endicott Home for the Retarded in Creston needed a gardener who could also help with kids. Lepine was hired.

The institution's name grates a bit today. But Dr. William Endicott, the founder, was committed to helping people with developmental disabilities live full lives in their communities, a pioneering vision at the time. The home's thirty children had been joined by the first adult residents a year earlier.

Things went well at first. Then Lepine started acting oddly. He drove off in one of the institution's trucks, without permission, and was fired.

And things unravelled. He harassed the staff, did time in a mental health facility in Cranbrook, but kept going back and bothering people at the Endicott Home. He landed in Riverview Hospital, the province's main mental health facility in Port Coquitlam, outside Vancouver.

Lepine didn't like it. He had unfinished business. On July 30, 1982, he walked away from the hospital. It wasn't hard. He had no history of violence and wasn't considered a high-risk patient.

He should have been.

Lepine was becoming convinced only he could save the world from a nuclear holocaust. He was especially worried about the children at the Endicott Home, with their mental handicaps. They needed him.

He made his way to Oliver, and got work picking apples. He broke into a home to get two weapons—a .22-calibre automatic rifle and .30-calibre rifle. He was ready for his mission.

On August 28, a pleasant Monday in the Okanagan, Lepine confronted Charles Wright, seventy-one, and William Potter, sixteen, as they worked on the irrigation system in an Oliver orchard. Wright was a Vancouver photographer, recognized for his postcard images. He was retired and living with the Potters, long-time friends.

Lepine shot both and dragged their bodies into their Land Rover. He headed north, driving about ninety kilometres into wilder country, and dumped their bodies beside a forest road in the Kootenay Boundary country east of Kelowna.

Just before noon, he drove the Land Rover into a campground on Damfino Creek. Two couples from Princeton in their sixties—Lester and Phyllis Clark, and Allan and Mildred Wilson—were camping on the beautiful creek. Lepine chatted with them, left for a few moments, and came back with his two rifles. He ordered them into the camper and opened fire, reloading three times.

All four were seriously wounded, but the men managed to drive sixty-five kilometres until they met a grader operator who could help them. Phyllis Clark, sixty-one, died before she got to the hospital.

But now the police were alerted. About twenty-five RCMP officers from throughout the region started a hunt for the killer.

Lepine was not done. He drove another sixty kilometres and encountered Herbert Thomas, fifty-seven, and his wife Nellie, fifty-six, near Edgewood, on the west shore of Lower Arrow Lake. He shot them, abandoned the Land Rover, and took their car.

Less than an hour later, twenty-four-year-old Thomas Pozney of Nakusp was coming off the lake after a day of fishing when he saw Lepine approach. He was the last to die.

One day, six dead.

The RCMP captured Lepine the next morning, about ninety kilometres away at Galena Bay. He didn't resist. When he appeared in court on Wednesday, he sat quietly in oversized green overalls as the name of each person he killed was read out.

Lepine was diagnosed as paranoid schizophrenic, and in 1974 found not guilty by reason of insanity and committed to a secure care institution for the criminally insane. He has never been released.

VIGILANTE INJUSTICE

Wong Foon Sing was peeling potatoes for lunch in the Shaughnessy mansion. It was July 26, 1924, a fiercely hot day for Vancouver. He heard a bang, like a car backfiring. But when he looked out the window, there was no one around.

Something seemed wrong.

Wong wiped his hands and went to check on Janet Smith, the twenty-two-year-old Scottish nursemaid who was ironing in the basement. Her nineteen-month-old charge was asleep upstairs. Fred and Doreen Baker, their employers, were both out, he at work, she shopping downtown.

Wong looked in the laundry room.

Smith was sprawled lifeless on the floor. A .45-calibre handgun and an iron lay beside her right hand; the ironing board stood nearby. Her head was a bloody mess.

The sunny twenty-two-year-old nursemaid was dead.

Wong didn't call the police or a doctor. He telephoned Frederick Baker in his downtown office.

Something is wrong with Nursie, he said.

*   *   *

Three people, three different paths to Vancouver.

Frederick Baker was pedigreed, a scion of two successful families. Doreen Smith, his bride, was the daughter of a Victoria businessman. After their marriage, they had lived in

London, then Paris, before returning to Vancouver and the import-export business. He belonged.

Janet Smith was working class, born in Perth, Scotland. Her father shovelled coal into steam engines. The family moved to London, and Janet studied to be a nursemaid. The Bakers hired her. They moved to Paris, then Vancouver, and Janet, promised thirty dollars a month, came along.

Wong Foo Sing's background in China is a mystery. He was twenty-seven, and had been in Canada since he was fourteen, working briefly in a Chinatown laundry before the Bakers hired him as a houseboy. He apparently had a wife and son in China, perhaps the result of a visit two years earlier.

Baker listened to Wong, then called police. The home was in Point Grey, a separate municipality with 14,000 residents and little crime. Point Grey wanted to become Vancouver's Nob Hill, a community for the rich and prominent. Two years earlier it had passed the first zoning bylaws in Canada to make sure shops wouldn't suddenly appear beside someone's expensive home.

The Point Grey police department's sixteen officers rarely faced major crimes, and knew it was their job to keep the prominent families happy.

Cst. Jim Green was the first on the scene. He saw Smith's body, in a blue nursemaid's uniform, her arms stretched above her head. He picked up the pistol, made note of a blood-spattered, broken pair of glasses. The iron beside her was still warm. There was a bullet hole just above her right eye, and a large exit wound in the back of her head.

Suicide, he immediately proclaimed. Instead of waiting for an autopsy—normal procedure—the police and coroner ordered the undertaker to embalm Smith's body right away.

Within days, the Point Grey police were accused of incompetence, or a cover-up. Rumours of every kind swept Vancouver. Smith had been murdered. Wong had done it. Baker. A mystery killer.

The story had all the right elements to be a sensation.

The Bakers were among the elite, in a time when Vancouver was sharply divided on class lines. Reports of trouble in the homes of the rich were eagerly consumed.

Janet Smith was a perfect heroine. She was young, cheerful, bright, an upright Scottish lass with a lively social life and lots of suitors, making her way in a new world. No one believed the attractive, sunny young woman would kill herself.

Poor Wong Foon Sing was close to the perfect suspect. Anti-Chinese sentiment—and racism—were the norm in Vancouver in 1924.

Chinese immigrants had been seen as a necessary evil, cheap labour to build the railways and work the mines. But by the mid-1880s, the railway work was done. In 1885, the first head tax—a fee collected from Chinese immigrants to deter immigration—was introduced. It was steadily raised, reducing immigration and preventing men from bringing over their families.

Even in the 1920s, newspapers warned of the "Yellow Peril." In 1923, a year before Janet Smith died, Parliament passed the Chinese Immigration Act, which virtually barred any new arrivals.

Chinese men—and the population was overwhelmingly male—were seen as opium-using, degenerate gamblers obsessed with white women.

Wong was a young man, tall, handsome, and well-dressed. He lived in a basement room; Smith lived two floors above. He was, apparently, alone in the house with her when she died. He was in a bad situation.

The *Vancouver Star*, owned by a political rival of the Baker clan, led the attack on the suicide verdict. Rumours raced through the city. Smith had been killed as a result of a wild party, and her murder was being covered up. She had been assaulted, one version went, or accidentally killed during a drunken fight between two guests. The imagined Jazz-Age lifestyles of the rich made for great speculation.

Revd. Duncan McDougall, an arch-conservative Scottish Presbyterian, was persuaded by a friend of Smith that she had been murdered. McDougall was controversial—he had recently announced his support for the Canadian Ku Klux Klan. (The next year, the Klan moved to headquarters in a Shaughnessy mansion about ten blocks from the scene of Smith's murder.)

But he had influence, and took his concerns to Vancouver's United Council of Scottish Societies. The council—politically powerful given the province's large Scottish population—successfully pressed for a new investigation.

The results were sensational. British Columbia Provincial Police Inspector Forbes Cruickshank quickly concluded Smith had been murdered and her body arranged to fake a suicide. There were no powder burns on her face, he noted, suggesting the gun had been fired from several feet away. Smith had no obvious way even to have the gun.

The fastest way to crack the case was to get answers from Wong, Cruickshank decided—whatever that would take. The police couldn't be directly involved in kidnapping, so he hired a private detective to snatch Wong on his weekly visit to Chinatown. Cruickshank was there for the questioning—and beatings—that lasted hours. Wong's story didn't change.

The police were getting nowhere. Public outrage was growing.

In late August, Attorney General Alexander Manson, pushed by the Scottish Societies, ordered a second inquest. Smith's body was exhumed.

The inquest was a sensation. Crowds pushed and scuffled with police to try to claim seats. A string of witnesses offered dramatic and contradictory evidence.

The largest crowd—some 1,500 people—showed up to try and claim a seat when Wong testified. Chinese witnesses did not usually take the normal oath to tell the truth on the witness stand.

But Alex Henderson, lawyer for the Scottish Societies, demanded Wong go through a bizarre swearing-in ritual that involved chopping the head off a chicken. He simply repeated the evidence he had already given.

On September 6, after five days of hearings, the jury delivered its verdict.

Janet Smith had been murdered.

The killer remained unknown. Rumours swirled about a wild party. About drug deals. (Baker's company dealt, legally, in opium and other drugs.)

And about Wong. One of Smith's fellow servants had testified she feared Wong. But her diaries said nothing of that, and noted he had given her presents, including a silk nightgown.

Evidence or not, racism and hysteria were rampant. The *Vancouver Star* called for greater protection for servants like Smith. "No young and pretty girl should be left alone and unprotected in a house with a Chinaman," it said. "It is against all rules of decency and safety." Vancouver MLA Mary Ellen Smith introduced a bill that would prevent white women from working in a home if there were Chinese servants. It failed to pass.

The unsolved case was an embarrassment. And on March 20, 1925, eight months after the murder, Wong was kidnapped once again, this time by police agents wearing white Ku Klux Klan hoods. He was held for six weeks in a Vancouver house, tortured and threatened. But he never changed his story.

On June 1, the kidnappers released Wong on a street where other Point Grey officers were waiting to arrest him for murder. (The kidnappers, it was later revealed, included Point Grey Police Department officers and officials from the Scottish Societies. Manson, the Attorney General, knew where Wong was being held but didn't act to free him.)

The charge was a sham. There was no evidence against Wong. The authorities hoped he might be holding back some information and would talk if threatened with a murder conviction and the death penalty.

But it didn't work. A grand jury dismissed the charge against Wong before it even went to trial.

Wong went back to working as a servant for the Bakers for a year, then returned to China. Frederick Baker continued as a member of Vancouver society.

And Janet Smith's murder remains a mystery.

WELCOME TO CANADA

Robert Dziekanski died on the polished floor of Vancouver's airport just after 1:00 a.m. on October 14, 2007, in front of a small and horrified audience.

Four RCMP officers had tasered him repeatedly, even as he lay on the ground.

When he stopped breathing, they stood around and waited for paramedics. None of the Mounties started CPR, or provided any assistance.

Dziekanski had arrived in the airport about ten hours earlier, ready to start a new life in Canada. His mother, Zofia, had worked two jobs in Kamloops to save enough money to bring her forty-year-old son to Canada from Poland. She was there at the airport to meet him.

But his flight was two hours late. He spoke no English, and had great difficulty clearing Immigration and finding his way through the airport. No one helped him as he wandered the arrivals hall.

No one helped Zofia either. She was told Robert wasn't in the airport. By 10:00 p.m., after waiting nine hours, she left.

Robert was frustrated, angry, and exhausted. He had travelled for nineteen hours and spent another nine hours trapped in the airport. He finally cleared Immigration at 12:45 a.m. But he still had no idea where to go.

And his frustration boiled over. Dziekanski was a big man. He had worked in construction and as a miner. He paced around, pushed a computer to the floor, and toppled a small table. Someone called for help.

So four RCMP officers—constables Gerry Rundel, Bill Bently, and Kwesi Millington, and supervisor Cpl. Benjamin Robinson—headed to the scene.

They didn't discuss any plan to deal with Dziekanski on the way to the terminal from their nearby detachment. They didn't try to find a translator. They didn't try to de-escalate what was a tense situation.

Instead, the four RCMP officers marched up to the immigrant. Stand against the counter, they ordered, and place your hands on top. And, although he didn't understand the words, Dziekanski moved to the counter, where he picked up a stapler.

About twenty-five seconds had passed since the Mounties arrived at the scene. Robinson ordered an attack with the taser, a device that delivers a 50,000-volt electric shock. Millington tasered Dziekanski, who immediately collapsed to the floor and went into convulsions. The four officers jumped on top of him and tasered him four more times. He stopped breathing.

The officers climbed off him and stood around for fifteen minutes, until paramedics arrived.

Dziekanski was alive, and had done nothing seriously wrong. He needed a skilled customer service representative, if anything.

Then four Mounties arrived, and in minutes he was dead.

But that's not what the RCMP told the public. Dziekanski, an RCMP spokesman said, pushed over his luggage cart and began screaming, pounding on windows, and throwing chairs and a computer to the ground.

That was not true.

Three RCMP officers working at the airport tried to calm him down, the RCMP told the media. "They couldn't make any rhyme or reason as to what he was doing," said RCMP Sgt. Pierre Lemaitre. "He kept yelling in what appeared to be a language from Eastern Europe."

That was not true.

"Unfortunately he didn't calm down. He kept being very aggravated. He grabbed an object off the desk, we're not sure what it was, and he continued to yell."

That was not true.

After the Mounties tasered Dziekanski, Lemaitre said, "He fell to the ground immediately although he continued to be very physically combative." It took three officers to hold hold him down as he was handcuffed, the RCMP claimed. "He continued to fight after that, still kicking and flailing and then lapsed into unconsciousness."

Untrue.

"We monitored his vital signs until medical emergency personnel could arrive."

Untrue.

Dziekanski was sweating profusely and violent, which could indicate either drug use or a medical condition, Lemaitre added.

But he wasn't violent. And might have just been hot and exhausted.

It was a long list of falsehoods. None of it was true.

And it might have gone uncontradicted.

But Paul Pritchard of Nanaimo, another traveller, was in the airport with his video camera. He captured the entire event.

Pritchard gave his camera and the memory chip to the RCMP that night to help with the investigation. They promised everything would be returned within forty-eight hours.

Pritchard got the camera back. Not the video. Evidence, the RCMP said. We will keep it as long as we want, maybe forever.

But Pritchard was troubled by the RCMP's false story and cover-up. He hired a lawyer, threatened to go to court, and got his video back.

On November 14, one month after Dziekanski was killed, Pritchard released the video to the media. And it showed that the official RCMP version of what had happened was untrue, a self-serving and utterly false series of fabrications.

Dziekanski wasn't resisting. The officers didn't try to talk to him. They tasered him repeatedly, crashed onto him, and killed him.

The video forced a reluctant British Columbia government to order an independent inquiry.

On June 18, 2010, the Braidwood Inquiry delivered its findings.

The RCMP was not justified in tasering Dziekanski. The four officers lied to investigators. The RCMP provided false accounts of the events, and failed to correct them even when it was clear they were false.

Too late for Robert Dziekanski, the burly Pole. He had been brutally killed.

Too late, of course, for his mother, Zofia.

And, for many Canadians, too late for the reputation of the RCMP.

JUROR ♥ GANGSTER

o surprise that Peter Gill was partying at the Pelican Bay disco on Granville Island.

Gill had every reason to celebrate. One week earlier, he had walked out of court a free man, beating two first-degree murder charges laid after the Dosanjh brothers were gunned down in a running Vancouver drug turf war.

It was an unexpected win for Gill and five "associates." A headline summed up the reaction to the jury verdict—"Dosanjh slayings acquittals stun police."

And no surprise that Gill chose Pelican Bay, or "Bay of Pigs" as it was unkindly known, a rough-and-ready hangout for Vancouver's high-profile gangsters in 1995.

But his date for the evening, she was a very big surprise.

An off-duty RCMP officer in the bar recognized the lavishly made-up, dramatically dressed blonde hugging and dancing with Gill.

It was Gillian Guess, a.k.a. "Elvira" or the "Dragon Lady." And Guess had spent the last eight months on the jury that decided Gill and company weren't guilty. Jurors and defendants aren't supposed to cuddle in clubs.

Police were already suspicious about Guess. An anonymous call to Crime Stoppers had alleged she was sleeping with Gill while she was on the jury.

Jurors in Canadian trials are generally quiet participants, anonymous and sworn to eternal secrecy.

Everyone noticed Guess. She sat in the front row of the jury box, in tight miniskirts or designer jeans and, some days, see-through blouses. High heels, bright red lipstick, big eye-lashes, and blonde hair often piled up to the sky. She had a striking resemblance to Patsy, the pouty-lipped, heavily made-up character from the British sitcom *Absolutely Fabulous*.

"Dramatic," Spencer Charest called her. Charest was a court reporter who hunched over a tiny keyboard, recording every word of the testimony. It took fierce concentration. But he noticed Guess.

Dramatic was a good word for the trial, too.

By 1994, the battle for Vancouver's hugely profitable drug trade had broken into open warfare. It was an ultra-violent, paranoid, highly armed world. The gangsters were a new breed, many from the IndoCanadian and Asian communities. They shared a style—close-cropped hair, flashy jewelry, expensive clothes, goatees, and muscles that came from hours at the gym. They rode in customized cars with bulletproof armour and hidden gun compartments. They flaunted their gangster status, taunted police with their boldness, and lived in a world of violence and betrayal.

Peter Gill and Bindy Johal, his brother-in-law, were at the centre of the gang world.

Police believed Johal, Gill, and four others were behind a machine-gun attack that killed Jimmy Dosanjh in February 1994 and, a few months later, another attack that got his brother Ronny. Gill and Johal, police believed, feared the Dosanjh brothers were coming after them and decided to strike first.

The investigation into the Dosanjh murders involved 150 officers and cost more than $1 million. The trial cost another $1.5 million.

So when Gill, Johal, and the others walked, police and prosecutors were embarrassed and angry. Defence lawyers accused police of using paid witnesses who lied. (The well-rewarded witnesses did appear to be making some of their evidence up as they went along.)

And Guess appeared on the TV news criticizing the police. Her face was blurred and her voice distorted, but anyone involved with the case knew it was her.

Police and prosecutors were desperate to know why they lost a case they thought they should win.

And they started looking at Guess, a thirty-nine-year-old divorced mother of two who had worked as a crime-victim counsellor in the North Vancouver RCMP detachment while studying for a master's degree.

Project Elvira, they dubbed the investigation. That was one of the nicknames courtroom staff gave Guess during the trial, a reference to a campy, bosomy character who hosted horror movies on TV as "Princess of the Dark."

Wiretaps and bugs placed secretly in her home—including her bedroom—gathered evidence. Police ended up recording some 18,000 conversations, and interviewed court staff, friends, and family.

In April 1997, Guess was charged with obstruction of justice for pushing the jury to a not guilty verdict.

And for the next eighteen months, British Columbians didn't need reality television. They had "The Gillian Guess Show."

Most defendants listen to their lawyer's orders and clam up. Not Guess. She had a steady stream of outrageous comments and quotes, and happily shared them.

The tone was set in an impromptu press conference after her first appearance on the charge. With her children—a son and daughter—by her side, Guess attacked and titillated. "They bugged my bedroom and they're bringing in evidence of Peter Gill and I having sex," she complained. "They spent hundreds of hours taping us having sex." (Later, Guess told a reporter she meant to say the police had spent hundreds of hours listening to the tapes. "I don't want to sound like I'm oversexed.")

"Who I sleep with is nobody's business," she said. "I'm afraid of the cops. They're absolute pigs."

That was just day one.

Court staff testified they had never seen anything like the flirting between Gill and Guess. "She would smile coyly and look seductive. It was a friendly, perhaps inviting look," a clerk said. Gill returned the attention, "almost seductive."

The relationship was so obvious that when Gill's wife, "Go-Go," came to court, she complained to a sheriff about the goo-goo eyes Guess was making at her husband.

Guess, twelve years older than the twenty-seven-year-old IndoCanadian gangster in designer suits, was even spotted talking with him outside the courtroom during a lunch break. Staff eventually took concerns to the judge. He raised the concerns with lawyers and defendants—but not with the jury.

Guess claimed innocence. She didn't have sex with Gill during the trial. No one said jurors couldn't have relationships with the defendants. And she did her job as a juror impartially. (She had at least one point. The juror's oath is an incomprehensible jumble of archaic legalese—"Do you swear that you shall well and truly try and true deliverance make between our Sovereign Lady the Queen and the accused at bar, whom you shall have in charge, and a true verdict give, according to the evidence, so help you God?")

* * *

But the evidence against her was overwhelming. A former friend said Guess confided that she was having an affair with Gill during the trial, sleeping with him in her North Vancouver home when her children were with their father. Gill called her from nightclubs and invited her to join him, the friend said, and they even met at the hotel where the jury was sequestered to reach a verdict. (The friend, a legal secretary, said she didn't come forward earlier because "Bindy Johal has a very bad reputation.")

Other jurors testified about their deliberations, unprecedented in a system that maintains absolute confidentiality about the jury process.

Guess was the only one who voted not guilty in their first straw poll, they said; four voted guilty and seven were undecided. Guess pushed for a not guilty verdict throughout the seven days of deliberations. She "was determined that they were all not guilty from Day 1," a juror testified. "If you did not agree with her opinion, heaven help you."

It looked at one point like the jury might not be able to reach a verdict, which could have resulted in a retrial. Guess claimed—falsely—that if the jury couldn't reach a verdict, then each juror would have to stand up in court and say how he or she voted. A chilling prospect in front of gangsters.

The trial was the best show in town, and Guess was the star both inside the courtroom, where she sometimes shouted at the prosecutor if she didn't like his questions, and outside, where she kept up a running, sometimes risqué, commentary. She even started her own website, with daily commentary on the trial, until the judge told her to knock it off.

It was hardly surprising that she paid attention to Gill, she told reporters. "After eight months, even the trial judge started looking good." Anyway, she announced, it was irrelevant whether she slept with Gill as long as she did her work as a juror properly. "It didn't matter if I had sex with all the accused and everyone in the public gallery—it's nobody's business."

For reporters, it was a gift that kept on giving. While the tapes of her and Gill having sex were never played in court, Guess offered a scoop to a news cameraman. "I've listened to the tapes and, you know, I'm pretty good."

On another lunch break, Guess compared herself to United States President Bill Clinton, then ensnared in the Monica Lewinsky sex scandal. If he could run the country given "his social life," she could be a good juror.

Even when she was found guilty of obstructing justice on June 20, Guess claimed her time on the evening news, defiant to the end.

"I have not committed a crime," she told reporters. "I fell in love, nothing more. At no time did I obstruct justice. You can't tell your heart how to feel."

The case was made for media. Guess knew it. "It's the original story of creation, it's about forbidden fruit. Then there's the interracial angle, the age difference, an older woman and a younger man, the element of danger, fear, sex, highly-charged emotions, murder, fashion, it's all there."

The two months between guilty verdict and sentencing were crammed with media coverage. Prime-time U.S. news shows, tatty daytime talk shows where the audience yelled at her son, magazines, film producers looking to buy the rights—the phone kept ringing.

And mostly, Guess said yes.

On August 20, she was sentenced to eighteen months in jail.

"May God forgive you," she dramatically said to the judge.

But the publicity never stopped. Guess served just thirteen weeks behind bars before being released on day parole. She posed for a magazine in her bathtub, shaving one raised leg, her electronic monitoring bracelet banding her ankle.

Two months later, Gill survived a drive-by shooting outside his house on a Sunday morning. He was eventually sentenced to six years for obstruction of justice for his relationship with Guess, based largely on her testimony.

Bindy Johal was gunned down in a nightclub five days before Christmas that year. His killers were never found.

None of the five surviving defendants in the Dosanjh murders was retried.

THE GOOD BOY KILLERS

Two bodies were sprawled in blood in the kitchen of the upscale Tsawwassen home. Doris Leatherbarrow was sixty-nine. Her daughter, Sharon Huenemann, was forty-three. Both had been hit in the head and their throats cut. The killers had covered the women's faces with dishcloths.

The crime scene made no sense. The home had been ransacked. But jewelry and cash were left behind. There were no signs of forced entry.

Four dinner places were set on the kitchen counter, with servings of lasagna in the microwave, ready to be heated.

The victims clearly knew their killers.

It was October 6, 1990. Police had two grisly murders and no obvious suspects, motives, or physical evidence like fingerprints.

They started talking to people. Leatherbarrrow ran four successful women's clothing stores. She had been involved in one serious dispute with a supplier, but there was no evidence linking him to the crimes.

Sharon Huenemann lived in Victoria, in beautiful and exclusive Ten Mile Point, with her husband Ralph, a University of Victoria professor. He had no obvious motive.

That wasn't the case for Darren, their eighteen-year-old son from Sharon's second marriage. His grandmother had done well in business, and in her will she split a $4 million estate between Darren and his mother. His mother's will left him everything. If both women died, Darren would be rich.

Darren was polite and charming, an A student and good-looking in a clean-cut teen kind of way. He was an enthusiastic actor in his high school theatre group, slated to play the lead in *Caligula*, the Albert Camus play about a Roman emperor who becomes a bloody murderer and abandons concepts of good and evil.

He had a rock-solid alibi. He had been home with girlfriend Amanda Cousins. His stepfather and Amanda both vouched for him.

And Darren didn't need the money. His grandmother was generous. When he was sixteen, she gave him a sporty $30,000 Honda Accord, and he had some $30,000 in the bank.

Police could only plod on as the trail grew colder, interviewing anyone who might help unlock the puzzle.

Almost three weeks after the murders, they got a break.

Officers interviewed Toby Hicks, a grade twelve classmate. Darren was obsessed with money, he said, always talking about his rich grandmother. He knew about the wills.

"If I kill granny, I get half her money, and if I kill my mom also, I get the other half," he had said to Hicks and others.

The perfect, polite teen became the prime suspect. The problem was his alibi.

If he was at home, who killed the two women?

Police started looking harder at Darren's friends. The students talked about him, and each other. David Muir, sixteen, and Derik Lord, seventeen, began to attract the officers' attentions. They were good students. There was nothing obvious to make police think they were capable of cold-blooded murder. But classmates mentioned that both collected knives, throwing stars, and other exotic weapons. The three played Dungeons and Dragons together, a role-playing fantasy game of exotic characters, plots, and battles.

Lord and Muir had alibis. They told police they were wandering around Victoria's small Chinatown the night of the killings, until Darren and his girlfriend, Amanda Cousins, picked them up. Darren and Amanda confirmed the story.

Police weren't satisfied. They traced the route Lord and Muir would have taken if they had travelled to Tsawwassen and killed the women, showing their pictures along the way. Both were distinctive, Muir with a square face and small features, Lord strikingly skinny and young looking.

It worked. A taxi driver said he might have seen Muir that night. Two boys had been playing football in a yard next door to the death house. One said he had seen Muir and Lord on the street that evening.

It wasn't much, but it was enough to get court approval for wiretaps on the three suspects. Once the phones were bugged, police went to Muir and told him they had witnesses putting him at the murder scene.

Then they waited.

It didn't take long for panicky, incriminating phone calls to start. "They know where we were on the 5th," Muir told Lord. "We've got to change our story."

They came up with a new alibi. Lord and Muir said they had gone to Tsawwassen, but just to buy knives to resell at school. They lied because they didn't want their parents to know they had left the island without permission. Huenemann and Cousins were just being good friends by lying for them. Very good friends, considering it was a murder investigation.

But things were unravelling. Police pressed Muir, who confessed everything. His signed statement was never used in court, because prosecutors decided police had offered him too good a deal. He would have served just three years for murder under the agreement police made.

But the statement let them increase the pressure on Amanda Cousins, Darren's girlfriend at the time of the killings. She had already been caught in lies, and police knew she had driven out to the ferry with Darren to pick up Muir and Lord when they came back from the killings. They threatened to charge her as an accessory to murder, and offered witness protection and a monthly $800 allowance.

And then the story came out.

Huenemann's talk about killing his mother and grandmother seemed like a joke to some people, but not a funny one.

With Lord and Muir, it became serious. Darren had big plans for the money, including making the school production of *Caligula* more spectacular. Arranging the murders would help him understand the character, too, he enthused.

They struck a deal. Muir and Lord would follow his careful plan for murdering his mother and grandmother. Once Huenemann collected the $3 million, he would buy Muir forty hectares of land and Lord a house. Each would get a $1,000 a month allowance.

Huenemann coached them through the plan and bought them crowbars and gloves. They should use the knives in the kitchen, he said, so it would look more like a robbery.

Getting in would be easy. Sharon knew the boys and would be glad to see them, even ask them for dinner, he predicted.

It unfolded exactly as Darren planned. The women did welcome the boys, and began to prepare lasagna. Muir thought that was funny, the victims cooking for the killers.

Then they pulled out the crowbars. Muir crushed Doris Leatherbarrow's skull and then cut her throat. Lord struck Sharon Huenemann, but he didn't swing as hard. As he leaned over her, struggling to find her jugular vein, she was still conscious.

"Why are you doing this?" she asked, seconds before her life ended. They placed the dishcloths on the women's accusing faces and left. Two teen killers, walking into the night.

Darren and Amanda were waiting when the duo got off the ferry. In the twenty-five-minute drive from the terminal, they talked about the killings.

Lord was quiet, brooding in the back seat. Muir was wired, joking, energetic. They all thought they had got away with murder.

They didn't. Once Cousins told the police what she knew, it was over. Huenemann was tried first, convicted, and sentenced to life in prison, with no chance of parole for twenty-five years. Lord and Muir were found guilty in a second trial and sentenced to life with parole eligibility in ten years.

It was justice. But it didn't explain how three teens, fine students with the world ahead of them, could become stone cold killers.

"Why are you doing this," Sharon Huenemann asked with her last breath. Her question was never really answered.

POSTSCRIPT

David Muir was paroled in 2002, granted day release on his first application.

Darren Huenemann remains in jail, not yet eligible to apply for parole. He briefly escaped in 1995 and was recaptured hours later.

Derik Lord has applied for parole every two years since 2002 and been refused every time. He continues to deny guilt. (His mother testified he was at home on the night of the killings.) The parole board believes that shows a lack of remorse and means he remains a danger. Lord's family has been consumed by the fight to prove his innocence since the night of the killings.

MARTYR OR MYTH?

I t took less than a minute. Dan Campbell and Ginger Goodwin came together in the hills above Cumberland, a scrappy Vancouver Island mining town. It was July 27, 1918.

Goodwin had been in hiding in the forests for three months, avoiding conscription and military service in the First World War. He was a union leader and socialist and didn't see why working people should be killing each other so capitalists could make money.

Campbell was a special constable, a hotel owner paid to help in the hunt for draft dodgers.

Campbell fired his hunting rifle. Goodwin fell dead. There were no witnesses.

Murdered, or martyred? Almost a century later, no one knows.

* * *

Albert "Ginger" Goodwin was thirty-one when he died. He had spent more than half his life in coal mines.

First in Yorkshire, where he followed his father into the mines when he was twelve, driving the pit ponies that pulled carts of coal to the surface. When Ginger—he had red hair—was fifteen, miners staged a two-year walkout. The owners evicted strikers' families from the grimy company row houses, including the Goodwins.

Canada, he decided, might offer better opportunities. At nineteen, he crossed the Atlantic and took work in a coal mine in northern Nova Scotia's Glace Bay. A new country, but the same struggles. In 1909, the miners were on strike in a bitter battle for union recognition, and families were again facing eviction and hunger.

Goodwin stuck it out through the strike, but in 1910 was on the move again, first to mines in British Columbia's East Kootenay region, then to Cumberland. The town was built practically on top of the mines. Mountains and the Comox glacier looked down on both the town and the Strait of Georgia a few kilometres away.

It was a beautiful setting, with the most dangerous mines Goodwin had seen. Methane gas seeped from fissures in the rocks. Explosions and fires took a terrible toll. During ninety-two years of operation, 295 men died—sixty-four in one 1901 disaster. Miners heaved a small sigh of relief any day they emerged, black-faced, from underground.

Goodwin liked the town, with its tidy rows of wood-framed company housing and its ramshackle Chinatown and Japantown, home to about 430 Asian miners. He was a skilled soccer player, and did well in the local league.

But in 1912, a major labour battle hit the mines. Goodwin was emerging as a union leader and a committed socialist. The two-year strike over union recognition failed—in part because of pressure to restore production as war loomed. But Ginger's role was noted. He was blacklisted by the mining company and left for Trail, where he worked in a smelter.

Goodwin was twenty-nine, short and slight, likeable and persuasive. He had decided that unions and socialism were the keys to better lives for working people. He was an activist, powerful speaker, and leader. In Trail, he was elected secretary of the union, vice-president of the British Columbia Federation of Labour, then a political arm for workers, and president of the Trail labour council. In 1916, he ran for MLA under the Socialist Party banner. It wasn't a token effort. In the previous election, socialists had captured twelve percent of the vote and won two seats. Goodwin came third, with about nineteen percent of the vote.

But another, bigger, issue was looming. By 1916, the war in Europe was more than two years old. Grinding trench warfare and new weapons brought massive casualties. Returning Canadian soldiers told horrific tales of life in the trenches.

Voluntary enlistment slowed just as more troops were needed. Conscription—the draft—was introduced in 1917.

Goodwin opposed the war, but registered and applied for an exemption to avoid service. (More than ninety percent of those who registered for the draft joined him in seeking an exemption.)

The doctors who assessed Goodwin found him a poor candidate for the military, with bad teeth and stomach problems. He was slight—even skinny—and had trouble eating. He received a temporary exemption from service. (Ill or not, he was still a star player for local soccer teams.)

Less than two weeks after a strike at the smelter began under Goodwin's leadership, he was ordered to report for re-evaluation and declared fit for service.

The smelter owners might have pulled strings to get an effective union leader out of the way. The military might have become more desperate for conscripts.

Either way, Goodwin wasn't having it. Instead of reporting for duty, he headed back to Cumberland and the woods. If the army wanted him, they would have to find him.

Goodwin wasn't alone. A small band of evaders, most local, took to the mountains west of Cumberland, helped by locals like Joe Naylor, a socialist and union activist who had been a mentor to Goodwin.

The Dominion Police was ordered to bring them in. It was no easy task. Local supporters helped the evaders, who knew the woods. For almost three months, officers had little success. They started hiring trackers and special constables.

Like Dan Campbell. He was a crack shot and skilled woodsman. He had been running a hotel outside Victoria since he had been kicked off the British Columbia Provincial Police for extorting a bribe from two women he caught recklessly driving a buggy.

On July 27, Campbell came upon Goodwin in the woods. Both men had rifles. Campbell said he called for Goodwin to surrender. Instead Goodwin raised his rifle.

So Campbell killed him.

Goodwin's friends and union leaders didn't believe it. They were convinced it was murder.

The authorities had suspicions as well. On July 31, Campbell was arrested and taken to Victoria.

That didn't defuse the mounting tension. In Cumberland, the mines were shut down, and a huge procession followed Goodwin's coffin to the cemetery.

In Vancouver, union leaders called a one-day general strike, and about 5,500 workers walked off the job, including longshoremen and shipbuilders. It was a day of violence, as returned troops opposed to the strike clashed with union members and denounced strikers as traitors.

A week after Campbell's arrest, he appeared before two justices of the peace. They were to decide if there was enough evidence to proceed with manslaughter charges. They heard that Goodwin's wounds—the bullet through his wrist and into his neck—were consistent with someone being shot while raising a rifle to shoot. But witnesses also said Campbell had talked about killing draft evaders. They decided there was enough evidence to justify a trial.

But in October, a grand jury heard the same evidence and reached the opposite conclusion. There would be no trial. Campbell walked out of the courthouse on Victoria's Bastion Square a free man.

And Ginger Goodwin became a symbol of workers' struggles in British Columbia.

COLD CASE

Jean Ann James and Gladys Wakabayashi might have seemed unlikely friends.

Gladys Wakabayashi was the forty-one-year-old daughter of a Taiwanese billionaire, thin and exotically beautiful, with long black hair and an easy smile. She lived with her twelve-year-old daughter, Elisha, in a 4,800-square-foot house in Shaughnessy, one of Vancouver's ritziest neighbourhoods. She studied, and taught, piano. Gladys never flaunted her family wealth. "Everyone we talked to said she was well-liked, kind and a compassionate lady," a police investigator recalled.

Jean Ann James was a flight attendant and union leader, perhaps a little chunky, with a blond perm, more than a decade older at fifty-three. Her husband, Derek, was an air traffic controller. They lived in a much more modest house in Richmond, comfortable, but not rich.

But Wakabayashi's daughter and James's son—both only children—were enrolled in the Tyee School in 1985. It was part of the Vancouver public system, a highly regarded Montessori school where parents took an active role.

The two couples met and quickly became friends. They socialized, had dinner gatherings in each others' homes, participated in school activities.

Danger can lurk when couples become close, especially when relationships change. Gladys and her husband, Shinji, drifted apart and separated, on good terms, in 1991. She was Chinese, he was Japanese, their daughter explained. "They didn't fight a lot. They just had cultural differences that couldn't be resolved."

And Gladys—beautiful, rich, musical, exotic—and Derek James found a strong connection. They became secret lovers.

Before long, Jean Ann James suspected.

She didn't confront them. Instead, Jean Ann began to play detective. She confided in the school janitor and borrowed his car so she could trail her husband undetected, but didn't catch him out. She called his hotel room when he was travelling on business, but Derek always covered his tracks and had explanations for absences.

So on June 15, 1992, she told a friend, Brendan Carver, about her suspicions. He worked for a research company, and she had him get the telephone records from her husband's hotel room on one of his weekend trips.

She instantly recognized the Wakabayashis' phone number. But once again, she was thwarted. Anticipating trouble, Gladys had asked her estranged husband to say Derek had been calling him.

Some people might have waited, or let it go, or confronted their husbands.

But Jean Ann James acted. On Wednesday June 24, as Vancouver sweltered under an unusual heat wave, she drove to Shaughnessy, parked a few blocks from the Wakabayashi house, and made her way there through back lanes. She had called her rival and said she had a present for her, and would meet her once their children were in school.

The friends had coffee in the kitchen, made small talk. They went upstairs. In the walk-in closet, Jean revealed her gift, a necklace.

Let me put it around your neck so you can see how beautiful it will look, she said. Instead, she slipped on gloves and, with a razor-sharp box cutter, slashed open Gladys's throat.

James was not yet done.

"Tell me the truth," she said. "And I'll call you an ambulance." She slashed her victim's legs, seeking a confession. How long had the affair been going on?

Then James, the suburban mom and flight attendant, washed the coffee cups and wiped away any evidence of her deadly visit. She dropped the weapon in a Dumpster on her drive home, disposed of her clothes in the school incinerator.

And her rival was gone.

Police were suspicious. They interviewed James. But they couldn't find evidence. It seemed the perfect crime.

But, sometimes, murder will out.

*　　*　　*

In 2007, fifteen years after the killing, the British Columbia Unsolved Homicide Unit—the cold case squad—pulled the file on Gladys Wakabayashi's murder, pored over the files, and decided only a confession could close the case. And they set out to get one.

The Mr. Big sting was pioneered by the RCMP in British Columbia. Police create a fictional world, lure the suspect into a criminal fantasy, and coax or coerce a confession.

By January 2008, police were ready to start the seduction of Jean Ann James. The play was written and the characters created, each with a backstory and role to play.

And the curtain went up.

Act One opened in the posh Spa Utopia in downtown Vancouver, with its waterfalls and faux Roman statues. Jean Ann James received a call saying she had won a day of treatments—although she couldn't remember entering any contests.

A stretch limo picked her up, and James found herself riding with another winner, the proudly nouveau riche wife of a developer. They talked in the limo and through a day of massages and pedicures and wine. By day's end, James had invited her new friend to join her and Derek at a wine-tasting at the Rosedale restaurant on Robson Street.

Except the new friend was really an undercover police officer. The spa day, the limo, the chance meeting, the tales of a free-spending lifestyle were the start of the sting.

They had fun at the wine-tasting, and on excursions to shop for gourmet foods and to Granville Island to wander and buy pastries. They shared details of their lives. James talked about her son, an aspiring actor, her dreams of more money and a house in Shaughnessy.

Then the curtain rose on Act Two. In March 2008, police created a "scenario." The new friend took a detour on an afternoon outing, stopping in the giant entrance plaza of the Sheraton Wall Centre Hotel. She parked, illegally, told James to watch the car, and grabbed a package to take into the hotel, returning without it. There was no explanation.

On another outing, the officer showed off three giant bundles of twenty dollar bills—at least $75,000. Soon, as they grew closer, James had to believe her new friend was involved in crime. "She's turned into one of the best friends I've had," she confided.

Soon, James went from observer to participant. After the pair lunched at the elegant Fish House in Staney Park one day, all bright windows and white linen tablecloths, her friend asked James to keep watch when she met someone. The officer/friend paid James $300.

A line was crossed. Now the goal was to drag James in deeper. Her new friend slowly confessed she was involved with organized crime, helping launder money at Vancouver casinos and selling stolen credit cards. She introduced James to fake gangsters, who talked more about their crimes. They lavished attention on her, paid for expensive meals and wine, and flaunted the money they were making.

But the criminals were all cops, the scenes all elaborately scripted, the cash from police coffers.

By October—nine months after James met her new friend at the spa—police were ready for Act Three. The gang said they needed to settle a score with a man who owed them $300,000, by kidnapping and beating him.

And James, the sixty-nine-year-old suburbanite, didn't blink at the battered victim, his injuries artfully created with makeup.

The deadbeat got off lightly, she told the new friends in crime. She would have cut off his fingers or burned his genitals with a curling iron or put raw meat on his crotch and let dogs at him.

Act Four introduced Mr. Big. The gang offered James a chance to earn a one-third share in a $700,000 score, and sweetened the deal with promises to use connections to help her son's acting career.

But first she had to meet the boss, Mr. Big, in Montreal. That's the decisive moment in the sting, when the suspect—to establish credibility, or out of fear—confesses.

On November 27, James knocked on the door of a suite at the Intercontinental Hotel in Montreal to meet Mr. Big, really an RCMP sergeant with a flair for undercover work.

She settled in an off-white loveseat in a dark sweater and grey pants, looking more like a grandmother than a gangster. Mr. Big was in an armchair half facing her, shined shoes, expensive-looking suit, and a file folder on his lap. Research, he would claim, on James's past.

It was an artful performance. Mr. Big talked about his thirty years at the top, the importance of trust, his unhappiness that his associates had brought James in on the deal without his consent, the need for violence sometimes. "It can get pretty sporty," he warned. He was looking, he said, for "A to Z" people who could do whatever was needed.

It was an audition and job interview, he said, and he was skeptical she would make the cut.

The encounter, captured by a hidden camera, did at first sound much like a job interview.

James, speaking with a faint British accent, ran through her work experience. She had trained as a nurse in England, she said, but became a flight attendant when her qualifications weren't recognized in Vancouver. She rose through the union ranks to become a national vice-president, but was "knifed in the back" in the rough world of union politics.

Finally, Mr. Big pulled a newspaper clipping about Gladys Wakabayashi's murder from his folder. His people in Vancouver had heard rumours about this, he said. Was she involved?

James hesitated. "This is strictly between you and I, right?"

And then she laid it all out. How she discovered the affair, planned the murder, slashed Wakabayashi's throat, then tormented her with more cuts, hid the evidence, told no one, and refused to answer police questions.

Mr. Big was impressed, interested. He kept probing for details. Incriminating details.

He asked if there was any evidence that could be used against her, anything she had taken from the home, because his Vancouver connections had heard the rich family was planning a civil suit and pressing the police for action.

"They got this in Vancouver, this cold case squad," he said. "You ever hear about that?"

And after an hour and forty minutes, James left the hotel room.

Shakespearean tragedies have five acts.

The curtain opened on the final act barely two weeks later, on December 12, when police knocked on the door of James's Richmond house, told her she was charged with first-degree murder, and led her away in handcuffs, leaving behind the Christmas display her neighbours so admired.

James was soon released on bail.

But when her trial began in October 2011, the confession to Mr. Big was a fatal piece of evidence. The defence battled valiantly. James's lawyers suggested other possible killers—the Chinese mafia, Wakabayashi's ex-husband, a plumber who had worked in the home. They questioned the confession to Mr. Big, noting James could have been frightened of the pretend gangster or making up stories to establish her credibility. They pointed to the lack of physical evidence.

None of that persuaded the jury. On November 4, they took only hours to find James guilty. She was sentenced to twenty-five years in prison without parole—effectively a life sentence. An appeal was unsuccessful.

The curtain had fallen. It took nineteen years, but the murder of Gladys Wakabayashi was solved.

LAST MAN HANGED

*L*eo Mantha ate his last meal—a T-bone steak. He wrote a letter to his sister, prayed with the priest, and then shuffled, in chains, to his date with the hangman.

His life ended on April 27, 1959, in a grim concrete shaft at Oakalla Prison. He was the last man hanged in British Columbia.

And he died because he was gay.

Homosexuality was illegal in the 1950s, seen as a sickness and perversion. Gays and lesbians knew to keep their lives and loves hidden.

Mantha was a product of that world. Born on December 22, 1926, he grew up in Verdun, a working-class suburb of Montreal. His family was devoutly Roman Catholic and he was an altar boy. But he knew he was different. When other boys started chasing girls, he went through the motions.

His world was jolted when he was twelve, and learned his family had been living a lie. The woman who he had been told was an older sister was, in fact, his mother. His grandmother had been pretending he was her child. He was never the same, an aunt testified at his trial.

Mantha made it through grade eight, then started work in a munitions plant as the Second World War ended.

He went on to work for the Canadian National Railway, first as an office junior and then in the railway's sprawling brick repair yards in Pointe St. Charles, a tough industrial neighbourhood.

He decided to join the Royal Canadian Navy and get out of Montreal. Mantha's occasional, tentative sexual adventures with men became much more frequent in foreign ports, all with hidden gay bars and clubs.

In San Francisco, during a shore leave that included a lot of drinking, Mantha misjudged his prospective partner. He woke up after a beating, with a raw head wound and lingering headaches, chills, and fevers. He decided to seek medical treatment in the navy hospital when his ship returned to Esquimalt.

That was a mistake. During "neurological tests," doctors discovered what they called his homosexual depression and feelings of "inferiority and inadequacy." The military was "the last place in the world for a man with this sort of conflict," the doctor's report concluded.

Mantha was honourably discharged, and quickly found work as an engineer on tugboats based in Victoria, living close to downtown in James Bay.

He was strong, rough-featured, with a broad, battered nose and a shock of dark hair rising up like a crown. There was a touch of the thug about him, to be sure, but a striking energy.

In the summer of 1958, a gay bartender at the Empress Hotel introduced Mantha to Aaron Jenkins, whom everyone called Bud.

Jenkins was in the navy, but hardly happily. He was seven years younger than Mantha, and enlisted in 1956 mainly because nothing else had worked out back in Coles Valley, Nova Scotia. He couldn't get into teachers' college and didn't like the low pay and long hours as a Royal Bank clerk. The navy was a way out.

But not an entirely successful one. Jenkins was initially unhappy, and surprised he couldn't just quit. An evaluation described him as "immature, highly effeminate and emotionally unstable." Jenkins was intelligent, but "quite unsuitable for service."

The two men had an intense affair through the summer, according to Mantha. A photo shows them in bathing suits, Mantha looking away from the camera and Jenkins—square-jawed, tousled hair—looking appraisingly at the photographer.

Then Jenkins tried to call it off and, according to Mantha, said he wasn't gay and was simply hustling Mantha for money. He said he planned to marry a girlfriend.

Mantha confronted Jenkins early on the morning of September 6, 1958, in his sleeping quarters in Nelles Block, a barracks building at CFB Esquimalt. Somehow Mantha made his way past sentries at the gate and on each floor of the barracks, and entered the room without waking Jenkins's roommates.

Minutes later, Jenkins lay bleeding, stabbed fatally in the throat. A bloody hunting knife with a five-inch blade was found in the barracks.

Navy officials suggested the death was a suicide. They wanted the case to go away.

But civilian police conducted a proper investigation, and a search of Jenkins's locker, and found love letters signed "All My Love, Leo."

It did not take long to track down Mantha, who confessed to stabbing Jenkins, but said he didn't intend to kill him.

Mantha's lawyer was George Gregory, an experienced counsel and a serving Liberal MLA.

When the trial began, Gregory set out to show this was a crime of passion, and not premeditated murder. The difference for Mantha was enormous—a lengthy prison term, or death by hanging.

When the trial ended, Justice John Ruttan gave the jury three options—not guilty, manslaughter, or murder.

They chose murder.

And in 1958, the automatic sentence was death.

But there was still hope for Mantha. While the law mandated capital punishment, the federal cabinet routinely commuted death sentences to life imprisonment. That was especially true in crimes of passion, where the killing was out of character.

Ruttan immediately wrote to the federal justice minister, Davie Fulton of Kamloops, saying that this was a crime of passion and strongly recommending clemency.

All he got in response was a telegram from Fulton. Mantha would hang.

Partly, Mantha was a victim of politics. The federal government had been routinely commuting death sentences, while continuing to proclaim its support for capital punishment. The issue was politically sensitive. Some executions had to be allowed to go ahead, or its support for the death penalty would look like empty posturing.

John Diefenbaker, the Conservative prime minister elected the year before, opposed the death penalty. He was a former defence lawyer and believed it was too easy for the state to kill an innocent person. His government commuted fifty-five out of sixty-three death sentences over the next six years. But he was not willing to take the risk of abolishing capital punishment. (That did not happen until 1975, in a 130-124 vote in Parliament.)

So someone had to die. Mantha spent 100 days awaiting execution in the same prison with Bob Chapman, a nineteen-year-old farm boy who had killed his older brother. The two were supposed to hang together.

But on April 24, three days before the scheduled hangings, the federal cabinet commuted Chapman's sentence to life imprisonment.

His first words to his mother were about Mantha's fate. "What about Leo. They won't do it to Leo, will they?"

Chapman and his family sent a telegram to Fulton, urging commutation. To no avail.

The other problem—the bigger problem—was that Mantha was gay. That meant inevitable prejudice and scorn at the idea of a crime of passion.

Lloyd McKenzie, who prosecuted Mantha, said twenty years later that Justice John Ruttan believed Mantha's sexual orientation was a strong factor in the government's decision to go ahead with the execution. "He had a very heavy load to carry in defending himself in this case because he was homosexual," McKenzie said. "There's no doubt about it, that was a very strong factor against him."

The case was even more sensitive because prejudice and Cold War paranoia had produced a campaign to identify and remove gays and lesbians in the military and intelligence services.

On April 26, Mantha and prison officials began preparing for his death. As the midnight hour of execution neared, a special phone line was kept open, awaiting a last-minute reprieve from Ottawa.

It never came.

Mantha entered the converted elevator shaft used for hangings. He had refused the sedation offered to condemned prisoners. His wrists were bound behind his back and his legs at the knees. His last sight, before the hood was pulled over his head, was hangman Camille Branchaud, the priest, and seven guards standing in a semicircle around him.

Witnesses—including Gregory, his defence lawyer, and two reporters—watched below.

At 12:08 a.m. on April 27, the executioner pulled a long wooden lever, the trap door opened, and Mantha fell. He hung for twelve minutes before being pronounced dead, the forty-fourth person executed in Oakalla. And the last.

Gregory, his lawyer, had been with him in his cell until fifteen minutes before the execution. Mantha died "a very brave man," the defence lawyer said.

POSTSCRIPT

The last two executions in Canada took place in December 1962. Beginning in 1963, the law remained in place but governments commuted all death sentences until 1976, when capital punishment was abolished.

McKenzie believed Gregory never fully recovered from the experience of unsuccessfully defending Mantha and witnessing the hanging. Gregory was appointed a British Columbia Supreme Court justice in 1964. He took his own life in 1973.

SOURCES

MILKSHAKE MURDERER—*Vancouver Province*; *Vancouver Magazine*; *British Columbia Murders*, Susan McNicoll (Heritage House, 2010); *At Home With History*, Eve Lazarus (Anvil Press, 2007); *Irrefutable Evidence*, Michael Kurland (Ivan R. Dee, 2009); RadioWest.ca; Gocampbellriver.com; Supreme Court of Canada.

CRAZY EDDIE—*Peachland View*; *Province*; *Victoria Times Colonist*; *Vancouver Sun*; *Ottawa Citizen*; *Toronto Star*; *Eighteen Bridges* (December 2013); BC Supreme Court records; BC Legislature Hansard.

THE INDIAN PROBLEM—*Vancouver Sun*; *Victoria Times Colonist*; *New York Times*; *Seeing Red: A History of Natives in Canadian Newspapers*, Mark Cronlund Anderson and Carmen L. Robertson (University of Manitoba Press, 2011); "Dan Cranmer's Potlatch," *Canadian Historical Review* (1992); Umista.ca; Royal BC Museum.

THE BIG CON—*Victoria Times Colonist*; *Vancouver Sun*; *National Post*; BC Securities Commission; BC Supreme Court records.

WOMEN WE KILLED—*Campbell River Courier-Islander*; *Vancouver Sun*; *Vancouver Province*; *Victoria Times Colonist*; *On the Farm*, Stevie Cameron (Knopf, 2010); BC Superior Court documents; *Forsaken: The Report of the Missing Women Commission of Inquiry*.

OFFICERS DOWN—*Globe and Mail*; *Kamloops Daily News*; *Alberni Valley Times*; *Vancouver Sun*; *In the Line of Duty*, Robert Knuckle (General Store Publishing House, 2005); Officer Down Memorial website (www.odmp.org); Royal Canadian Mounted Police (www.RCMP.GRC.gc.ca); RCMP Veterans' Association.

KIDNAPPED—*North Shore News*; *Abbotsford Times*; *Vancouver Sun*; *Vancouver Province*; *Victoria Times Colonist*; BC Superior Court documents.

HOCKEY ON TRIAL—*Vancouver Sun*; *Vancouver Province*; *Bergen County Record*; *Sports Illustrated* (February 22, 2000; November 20, 2000); Dropyourgloves.com; YouTube; BC Superior Court documents.

SEX ON-CAMERA—*Vancouver Sun*; *Vancouver Province*; *Victoria Times Colonist*; *The Tyee*; BC Legislature Hansard; BC Civil Liberties Association archives; *Bill Bennett*, Bob Plecas (Douglas & McIntyre, 2006); *Scandal!!*, William Rayner (Heritage House, 2001).

GENTLEMAN OUTLAW—*British Colonist*; *Victoria Times Colonist*; *Vancouver Province*; RCMP online archives (www.rcmp-grc.gc.ca/hist/archiv-eng.htm); *The Grey Fox*, Mark Dugan and John Boessenecker (University of Oklahoma Press, 1992); *Interred With Their Bones*, Peter Grauer (Tillicum Press, 2006); *Old Bill Miner*, Frank Anderson (Heritage House, 2001).

WAITING DEMONS—*Victoria Times Colonist*; *Guardian*; *Vancouver Sun*; *Ottawa Citizen*; *The Stopwatch Gang*, Greg Weston (Macmillan, 1982); *Crowbar in the Buddhist Garden*, Stephen Reid (Thistledown Press, 2012).

THOSE MCLEAN BOYS—*British Colonist*; *Winnipeg Free Press*; *Dictionary of Canadian Biography*; *The Bad and the Lonely*, Martin Robin (Lorimer, 1976); *B.C. Provincial Police Stories*, Vol. 3, Cecil Clark (Heritage House, 1995); BC Metis Mapping Project (ubc.bcmetis.ca).

VANISHED—*Vancouver Sun*; *Victoria Times Colonist*; *National Post*; BC Superior Court documents.

MURDER AT SEA—*Vancouver Sun*; *Victoria Times Colonist*; *Toronto Star*; Associated Press; *Fatal Cruise*, William Deverell (McLelland and Stewart, 1991); BC Superior Court documents.

THE BOOGEYMAN—*Vancouver Sun*; *Victoria Times Colonist*; *Calgary Herald*; *Globe and Mail*; *Macleans*; BC Superior Court documents.

DEADLY MASSACRE—*The Chilcotin War*, Rich Mole (Heritage House, 2009); The Spirit of Pestilence (online); *BC Studies* (Winter 1982/83); Colonial correspondence, Court documents, Inquests, Letters (From canadianmysteries.ca).

THE ROCKEFELLER CON—*National Post*; *Vancouver Sun*; *Vancouver Province*; *Daily Telegraph*; *New York Times*; *Whistler Pique*; *Vanity Fair* (January 2001).

THE BEAST—*Toronto Star*; *Toronto Sun*; *National Post*; *Globe and Mail*; *Vancouver Sun*; *Where Shadows Linger*, William Holmes, with Bruce Northorp (Heritage House, 2000).

FORGIVENESS—*Squamish Chief*; *Whistler Pique*; *Abbotsford Times*; *Vancouver Sun*; *National Post*; *Victoria Times Colonist*; *Vancouver Courier*; *Walking After Midnight*, Katy Hutchison (Raincoast Books, 2006); BC Superior Court documents.

WHOSE BODY IS THIS?—*Ottawa Citizen*; *Vancouver Sun*; *Victoria Times Colonist*; *A Timely Death*, Anne Mullens (Knopf, 1996); CBC; BC Superior Court documents; Supreme Court of Canada judgment.

SMUGGLERS AND DEATH—*British Colonist*; *Nanaimo Bulletin*; *Gunboat Frontier*, Barry Gough (University of British Columbia Press, 1984); *William Duncan of Metlakatla: A Victorian Missionary in British Columbia*, Jean Usher (UBC doctoral thesis, 1969); *Colonial Despatches: The colonial despatches of Vancouver Island and British Columbia 1846-1871*, University of Victoria (bcgenesis.uvic.ca).

STEALING THE WORLD—*Vancouver Province*; *Victoria Times Colonist*; *Chicago Tribune*; *Outside* (June 1997); *The Island of Lost Maps*, Miles Harvey (Random House, 2000).

HOCKEY NIGHT—*Vancouver Sun*, *Buffalo News*, *Sports Illustrated* (May 11, 1987); *Toronto Star*; *Leaving Dublin*, Brian Brennan (Rocky Mountain Books, 2011); *Gross Misconduct*, Martin O'Malley (Penguin, 1989).

MAYDAY, MAYDAY, MAYDAY—*Alaska Highway News*; *Toronto Star*; *Edmonton Journal*; *Winnipeg Free Press*; *Montreal Gazette*; *100 Mile House News*; *The View From Seven* (http://theviewfromseven.wordpress.com); GenDisasters (www3.gendisasters.com); Aviation Safety Network.

GO HOME!—*Vancouver Sun*; *Victoria Times Colonist*; *Globe and Mail*; CBC; *Migrant Smuggling: Canada's Response to a Global Criminal Enterprise*, Benjamin Perrin (McDonald-Laurier Institute: True North in Canadian Public Policy, October 2011); "Opinion Discourse and Canadian Newspapers: The Case of the Chinese 'Boat People,'" Joshua Greenberg, *Canadian Journal of Communication* (2000).

SUBURBAN TERRORISTS—*Toronto Star*; *Vancouver Sun*; *Vancouver Province*; *Victoria Times Colonist*; *Équipe de recherche sur le terrorisme et l'anterrorisme*, "Direct Action (the "Squamish Five")," Julie Vinet (www.erta-tcrg.org/groupes/directaction.htm); *Direct Action: Memoirs of an Urban Guerrilla*, Ann Hansen (Between the Lines Books, 2001); *Fury's Hour*, Warren Kinsella (Random House, 2005); BC Superior Court documents; YouTube (Rosie Rowbotham/Brent Taylor interview).

BOMB ON A TRAIN—*Nelson Star*; *Nelson Daily News*; *Vancouver Province*; Doukhobor Genealogy (www.doukhobor.org); Inquest and investigator reports; Great Unsolved Mysteries in Canadian History (canadianmysteries.ca).

ESCAPE TO THE WILD—*British Colonist*; *Kamloops Standard*; *Toronto Star*; *Vancouver Sun*; *Trapline Outlaw*, David Ricardo Williams (Sono Nis Press, 1982); *The Bad and the Lonely*, Martin Robin (Lorimer, 1976); *Call in Pinkerton's: American Detectives at Work for Canada*, David Ricardo Williams (Dundurn Press, 1998).

TERROR IN THE SKY—*Vancouver Sun*; *Globe and Mail*; *Victoria Times Colonist*; *New York Times*; *Birmingham Mail*; CBC; *Loss of Faith*, Kim Bolan (McLelland and Stewart, 2005); Air India Commission Final Report; BC Superior Court documents.

GANGLAND EDEN—*Globe and Mail*; *Toronto Star*; *Vancouver Sun*; *The Mulligan Affair*, Betty O'Keefe and Ian Macdonald (Heritage House, 1997); *The History of Metropolitan Vancouver*, Chuck Davis (Harbour Publishing, 2011); *Jailed for Possession*, Catherine Carstairs (University of Toronto Press, 2006); *Webster!*, Jack Webster (Douglas& McIntyre, 1990); BC Government Liquor Policy Review (engage.gov.bc.ca/liquorpolicyreview/history); *Past Tense Vancouver Histories* (pasttensevancouver.wordpress.com); BC Radio History (bcradiohistory.radiowest.ca).

THE FALLEN BISHOP—*Vancouver Sun*; *Vancouver Province*; *Ottawa Citizen*; *Globe and Mail*; *They Called Me Number One*, Bev Sellars (Talon Books, 2013); Four Worlds International Institute; BC Superior Court documents.

SAVING THE CHILDREN—*Vancouver Sun*; *Vancouver Province*; *Spokane Daily Chronicle*; *Ottawa Citizen*; *Lethbridge Herald*; *Montreal Gazette*; Vancouver Postcard Club newsletter.

VIGILANTE INJUSTICE—*Daily Colonist*; *Vancouver Sun*; *Who Killed Janet Smith?*, Edward Starkins (Macmillan, 1984); *Vancouver Past: Essays in Social History*, ed. Robert A. J. McDonald and Jean Barman (University of British Columbia Press, 1986); *Dictionary of Canadian Biography*; *BC Studies* (Spring 1999).

WELCOME TO CANADA—*Vancouver Sun*; *Vancouver Province*; *Globe and Mail*; *Toronto Star*; Braidwood Inquiry Final Report.

JUROR ♥ GANGSTER—*Vancouver Sun*; *Vancouver Province*; *Globe and Mail*; *Toronto Star*; BC Superior Court documents.

THE GOOD BOY KILLERS—*Victoria Times Colonist*; *Vancouver Sun*; *Toronto Star*; BC Superior Court documents; *Such a Good Boy*, Lisa Hobbs Birnie (Macmillan, 1992); Canadianinjustice.com.

MARTYR OR MYTH?—*Globe and Mail*; *Vancouver Province*; *Daily Colonist*; "Plots, Shots, and Liberal Thoughts: Conspiracy Theory and the Death of Ginger Goodwin," Mark Leir, *Labour/Le Travail* (Spring 1997); *Fighting For Dignity: The Ginger Goodwin Story*, Roger Stonebanks (Canadian Committee on Labour History, 2004); *Ginger*, Susan Mayse (Harbour Publication, 1990).

COLD CASE—*Vancouver Sun*; *Vancouver Province*; CBC; BC Superior Court documents.

LAST MAN HANGED—*Montreal Gazette*; *Vancouver Province*; *Victoria Daily Times*; *The Canadian War on Queers*, Gary Kinsman (UBC Press, 2010); *William R. McIntyre: Paladin of Common Law*, W. McConnell (McGill-Queen's University Press, 2000); *Nathaniel Christopher: The Random Reflections of a Vancouver Journalist* (www.nathaniel.ca).

PHOTO: COURTESY THE AUTHOR

ABOUT THE AUTHOR

Paul Willcocks is a journalist with over 30 years of experience. He has won a Michener Award, been the recipient of a Jack Webster Award for being British Columbia's best columnist, and has been a National Magazine Writing finalist many times.